The Barnes & Noble

Cookie

BAKE-OFF

The Barnes & Noble

Cookie

BAKE-OFF

TOP 75 RECIPES FROM AROUND THE COUNTRY

STERLING
New York

STERLING

New York

An Imprint of Sterling Publishing
1166 Avenue of the Americas
New York, NY 10036

Principal photography by Bill Milne
Food styling by Diane Vezza

ISBN 978-1-4549-1745-8

Distributed in Canada by Sterling Publishing
c/o Canadian Manda Group, 664 Annette Street
Toronto, Ontario, Canada M6S 2C8
Distributed in the United Kingdom by GMC Distribution Services
Castle Place, 166 High Street, Lewes, East Sussex, England BN7 1XU
Distributed in Australia by Capricorn Link (Australia) Pty. Ltd.
P.O. Box 704, Windsor, NSW 2756, Australia

For information about custom editions, special sales, and premium
and corporate purchases, please contact Sterling Special Sales
at 800-805-5489 or specialsales@sterlingpublishing.com.

Manufactured in Canada

2 4 6 8 10 9 7 5 3 1

www.sterlingpublishing.com

THANK YOU FOR GIVING
US A TASTE OF HOME
AND SHARING YOUR
RECIPES WITH US!

CONTENTS

PART 1
SUGAR & SPICE

PART 2
SWEET & SAVORY

PART 3
CHOCOLATE

INTRODUCTION

My fondest memories as a child are connected to the kitchen. The kitchen is where I would spend hours with my grandmother, watching her create amazing meals from scratch. It is also the first place everyone would go when they walked in the door. It was pretty magical to see her working with those ingredients; she didn't just turn them into meals, she somehow turned them into experiences for the whole family. My grandmother's kitchen is where my love of food and my passion for creating such experiences with food truly began.

I have been a chef in many different types of kitchens over the years, from pizzerias, bars and grills, to fine-dining restaurants. One of the things I learned is that there is no better place for recipes to be sourced than the home kitchen. When you cook in a commercial environment, you cook to please the particular type of clientele, but when you cook in the home kitchen, you cook for yourself, your family and friends, or simply for the joy of cooking. The guiding essentials for those recipes are your tastes, your preferences, even your memories. Eating a home-cooked meal gives you a taste of that cook's favorite flavors, as well as a taste of that person's home.

With the Barnes & Noble Cookie Bake-Off Contest, I wanted to celebrate all those flavors of family and home, as well as one of my favorite dishes . . . cookies! There's something so amazing about taking a cookie recipe created in your kitchen and sharing it and your story with people around the country who are partaking in the same way. With this contest we were able to leverage the power of our cafés and Sterling Publishing to share these experiences with the most important people to us, our customers.

It was no easy task choosing the 75 recipes to include in this book, let alone the winner and runners-up. With over 4,000 entries from across the country, how could the decision be easy? Although I had to make hard choices, I couldn't be happier with the variety of recipes, stories, and overall response we received. I'm especially thrilled to have had the support of a group of leading chefs to help judge this very exciting contest. These 75 recipes represent everything I love about cooking and family—they're warm, inviting, and can't help but make you smile. I want to thank everyone who entered the contest, especially our finalists.

Jason Giagrande

Joey Campanaro (The Little Owl)

Joey Campanaro was raised in Philadelphia, where the food of his childhood inspired him to make cooking his vocation. With a culinary approach firmly rooted in his Italian grandmother's kitchen and honed in a range of America's top restaurants, Joey brings a lifelong affinity for Mediterranean cuisine to every dish he creates. Campanaro is the owner and chef of the Little Owl and the Little Owl—The Venue, which has received wide acclaim from critics and guests alike, including a two-star review from the *New York Times*, appearances on everything from *Iron Chef America* to the *Today Show* and the *Martha Stewart Show*, and continued buzz as one of New York City's most exciting restaurants. Campanaro is also the owner of the successful Blackfoot Consulting and the restaurants Market Table and the Clam.

Jonathan Waxman (Barbuto)

Working as a successful chef, restaurateur, and author, Jonathan Waxman has graced such prestigious kitchens as Chez Panisse in Berkeley and Michael's in Los Angeles. Waxman went on to open his own restaurant in New York City, Jams, described by the *New York Times* as "a culinary comet," as well as the famed Washington Park. Today, Waxman is the chef and owner of Barbuto in Manhattan's West Village. His first cookbook, *A Great American Cook*, was published in 2007 and his second book, *Italian My Way*, was released in April 2011.

Heather Miller (Barbuto)

Heather Miller is pastry chef at Barbuto in New York City. She has worked with Jonathan Waxman for many years, both at Barbuto and Washington Park. She was also pastry chef at Cookshop and AZ in New York, and Rialto in Cambridge, Massachusetts. Heather lives in Brooklyn with her husband and three sons.

Johnny Iuzzini (author of *Dessert FourPlay* and *Sugar Rush*)

Award-winning pastry chef Johnny Iuzzini hails from the Catskills region in upstate New York. A graduate of the Culinary Institute of America with more than twenty years of kitchen experience, Iuzzini honed his craft at highly lauded dining locations such as the River Café in Brooklyn, New York, along with Daniel, Payard, Café Boulud, and Jean-Georges in New York City. In 2006, the James Beard Foundation awarded Iuzzini "Pastry Chef of the Year." In addition he has been recognized as one of the "10 Most Influential Pastry Chefs in America" by Forbes, "Best New Pastry Chef" by *New York* magazine, and one of the "Top 10 Pastry Chefs in America" two years in a row by *Pastry Art and Design*. He was the head judge of Bravo's culinary competition series *Top Chef: Just Desserts*. Since leaving Jean-Georges, Iuzzini has started his own pastry and culinary arts consulting company, aptly named Sugar Fueled Inc. He is the author of *Dessert Fourplay: Sweet Quartets from a Four-Star Pastry Chef*.

Sharon Vanegas (The Red Cat)

Queens native Sharon Vanegas followed her childhood dream of working in the restaurant industry when she entered the Art Institute of New York City in 2002. She graduated two years later with an associate's degree in restaurant management and culinary arts. Vanegas landed her first pastry position at Spice Market and began a culinary journey through some of New York City's top kitchens, including Buddakan and Cesare Casella's Il Ristorante Salumeria Rosi, where she, after what she refers to as "pastry boot camp," became the restaurant's pastry chef. She also worked at Bobby Flay's Mesa Grill and joined him as part of the opening team for Gato. Vanegas's professional journey included time aboard working at restaurants in the Dominican Republic and China, finding inspiration in native ingredients, culinary traditions, and flavors. Vanegas joined the team at Jimmy Bradley's acclaimed restaurant the Red Cat as pastry chef in 2014, showcasing a seasonally inspired pastry program with her signature rustic yet elegant twist.

Jimmy Bradley (The Red Cat)

The author and chef-owner of the Red Cat, Jimmy Bradley presides over a neighborhood joint that has become a destination for guests from around the city and the country. A purveyor of straightforward, occasionally irreverent food and contagious conviviality, all of it wrapped up in an attitude-free package, Bradley has helped contemporary diners rediscover the intrinsic value of classic Mediterranean cuisine, reinterpreted for a modern American clientele. He and his recipes are regularly featured in the *New York Times*, *Food and Wine*, *Bon Appétit*, *Esquire*, and other food publications, as well as on local and national television programs, including the *Today Show*, *Top Chef Masters*, and the *Martha Stewart Show*. His first cookbook, *The Red Cat Cookbook*, was published by Clarkson Potter in fall 2006.

Sandy Solmon (CEO and Founder of Sweet Street Desserts)

Sandy Solmon is the CEO and R&D director of Sweet Street and leads a team of nine like-minded, passionate R&D pastry chefs. Based in Reading, Pennsylvania, Sweet Street now bakes for restaurants in over 60 countries and on every continent. Enjoyed throughout the day, and in every restaurant segment, Sweet Street products have delighted Barnes & Noble Café customers for over fifteen years. Among café favorites are her giant cookies, like the Chocolate Chunk, Peanut Butter with Reese's and her latest invention, the Salted Caramel Crunch. Sandy is married to Douglas Messinger, who runs Sweet Street's international business, and has a foodie daughter, Zoe, who just graduated from Cornell School of Hotel Administration, and, by the way, published her own cookbook, *Foodie Two Shoes*, while in high school.

Gennaro Pecchia and Alan Watts

Gennaro Pecchia and Alan Watts are the Men Who Dine, and their mission is to bring you inside the best and most authentic restaurants, bars, lounges, and all things food related in their own unique way! They are not conventional restaurant critics, but rather they are an underground foodie force—connecting with chefs, restaurants, and events through social media, word of mouth, and lots and lots of meals. The Men Who Dine actively seek out the greatest in food and eat their way through restaurants and events around the country. Each has a culinary background, and they are hooked up with and hooked into the best and brightest in food culture to inform their audience where the best eats are. If a restaurant makes it on their list of "Where We Dine," it is certainly not to be missed.

TRIPLE GINGER SPICE CRINKLES
KIT FORCEY, CALIFORNIA

Kit's passion for cooking and baking began at an early age when she started helping her mom and older sisters in the kitchen. Decades later, she is still dreaming up new recipes and drawing inspiration from the world around her. She has always been inspired by Julia Child, Ina Garten, Rachael Ray, and Giada De Laurentiis. Baking is more than just a creative outlet or a hobby for Kit—it's one of the ways she shows love to friends and family. There are few better feelings than the joy one gets watching a latest kitchen experiment disappear before her eyes! Kit always says to use your palate and take risks in all of your culinary adventures. She lives in San Jose, California.

THE RUNNERS-UP!

OMG COOKIES
SANDY AREVALO, ILLINOIS

Baking has always been a large part of Sandy's life, with sweet memories of time spent in the kitchen alongside her great-grandmother. So it's no surprise that what started as a hobby after her son was born, baking for her family and friends, eventually turned into a thriving business. In addition to her growing list of celebrity clients, Sandy has also donated countless sweets for Operation Shower, a nonprofit organization that provides baby showers to military wives whose husbands are deployed. Sandy currently resides in Crystal Lake, Illinois, with her husband and two kids.

COFFEE BREAK
BECKY SCHENCK, TEXAS

Becky was born and raised in central Illinois where, growing up, she spent most of her time with her grandparents. Her grandmother was the person who taught her to bake. Becky spent almost forty years working in the food-service business, and married in 1986. Life moved fast with little time to bake. In 2012, she relocated to Houston, Texas. She decided not to go back to work and found herself with more time to cook and bake. Now Becky has the time to spend with her husband and to enjoy all the things she loves to do!

 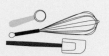

WINNING RECIPE!

TRIPLE GINGER SPICE CRINKLES

This recipe started with my sister's gingersnap recipe from before I was born. They came out kind of chewy, which we liked, but I thought they needed more spice and more crunch. I got the idea for the spice from my pumpkin bread recipe and adapted it for the cookies. Once I made these, they were a hit and one for the family recipe book.

**WINNER: KIT FORCEY
SAN JOSE, CA**

2¼ cups all-purpose flour
 2 teaspoons baking soda
 2 teaspoons ground ginger
 1 teaspoon fresh grated ginger
 1 teaspoon ground cinnamon
 ¼ teaspoon ground cloves
 ¼ teaspoon ground coriander
 ¼ teaspoon ground nutmeg
 ½ teaspoon salt
 ¾ cup butter, softened
 1 cup packed dark brown sugar
 ⅓ cup molasses
 1 large egg
 3 tablespoons chopped crystallized ginger
 Turbinado sugar for rolling

Preheat the oven to 375°F. Line baking sheets with parchment paper or silicone baking mats.

In a medium bowl, stir together the flour, baking soda, both ground and fresh ginger, cinnamon, cloves, coriander, nutmeg, and salt. In another bowl, using an electric mixer or stand mixer with the paddle attachment, mix the butter and brown sugar until fluffy. Add in the molasses and egg and beat until well blended. Stir in the flour mixture and crystallized ginger until combined. Cover with plastic wrap and refrigerate until firm, about 2 hours.

Using a tablespoon cookie scoop or ice cream scoop, shape dough into 1 inch balls. Roll the balls in the turbinado sugar to coat and place the balls 1 inch apart on prepared baking sheets. Sprinkle the tops with more sugar. Bake until the centers of the cookies are barely dry, about 9–10 minutes. It's okay if the cracks look wet; do not overbake. Let the cookies cool on the baking sheets for about 5 minutes, then transfer to a wire rack to cool completely.

SPIKED CHAI EGGNOG
Cookies

I absolutely love chai tea, and I love eggnog! I ate some regular eggnog cookies with a cup of chai tea and had an epiphany: The combination tasted so good, what if I combined the two and created an entirely new cookie? So I went to work blending the two together, and at the last minute, I decided to add in a splash of dark rum to bring out more flavors. It was such a great idea! It took a lot of trial and error (the first batch I made was flatter than pancakes), but I finally created the best balance of chewiness and a soft center.

CONTESTANT: LAUREN GARDNER
NORFOLK, VA

½ cup unsalted butter, melted
1¼ cups granulated sugar
1 packet of chai tea
1 large egg
2 tablespoons eggnog
Dash of salt
1 tablespoon dark rum
1 tablespoon vanilla extract
2 cups all-purpose flour
¼ teaspoon baking powder
¼ teaspoon baking soda
¼ teaspoon ground nutmeg
¼ teaspoon ground cinnamon
Decorating sugar

Mix the melted butter and sugar. Cut open the packet of chai tea and empty it into the mix. Mix in the egg, eggnog, salt, rum, and vanilla.

In a separate bowl, mix the flour, baking powder, baking soda, nutmeg, and cinnamon. Add the dry ingredients to the wet ingredients a little at a time, being careful not to overmix (overmixing will cause the cookies to be too puffy). Wrap tightly and refrigerate for 2–3 hours or freeze for at least 1 hour.

Preheat the oven to 350°F.

Line a baking sheet with parchment paper or a silicone baking mat. Scoop tablespoonfuls of the dough, dip into your desired color of decorating sugar, and place onto the baking sheet.

Bake for 15–16 minutes or until the tops appear crackled and the edges begin to brown. Remove from the oven and cool on the baking sheet for about 1 minute, then transfer to a wire rack and cool for 10 minutes.

Arabian Nights
CHOCOLATE FANTASIES

I created this recipe based on a story that goes, "In a glistening white palace in Moorish Spain, a beautiful, learned woman sat in the shade of a fragrant orange tree and told fantastic stories of genies, rocs, and ghuls. The caliph listened, rapt, entranced by the tales she spun. As he reclined, lost in a world of magic and mystery, he reached for a tray of sweet delicacies. Again and again, he bypassed the honeyed baklava, the sugared dates, and the delicate ladyfingers and came to rest on these delicious morsels. Their taste reminded the caliph of the beautiful storyteller."

CONTESTANT: FELICE BOGUS
RALEIGH, NC

- ¼ cup all-purpose flour
- ¼ teaspoon baking powder
- ⅛ teaspoon salt
- 2 eggs
- ⅔ cup granulated sugar
- 1½ teaspoons brewed espresso
- 1 teaspoon vanilla extract
- 2 tablespoons unsalted butter
- 5 ounces bittersweet chocolate (at least 70%), chopped
- 2 ounces unsweetened chocolate, chopped
- 2 tablespoons Aleppo pepper
- ¾ teaspoon ground cinnamon
- 14 caramel candies, unwrapped, or 4 ounces block caramel, chopped
- 1 tablespoon heavy cream
- ¼ teaspoon orange oil

Preheat the oven to 375°F and line two baking sheets with parchment paper or silicone baking mats.

In a small bowl, whisk together the flour, baking powder, and salt. Set aside.

With an electric mixer or stand mixer, beat the eggs for a few seconds to begin blending. Add the sugar, espresso, and vanilla and beat on high speed for 15 minutes, until the mixture is very thick.

Meanwhile, melt the butter and both chocolates in the top of a double boiler or a heat-proof bowl set over a saucepan of simmering water. Stir in the Aleppo pepper and cinnamon and continue stirring until smooth. Remove the bowl from the heat.

Fold the chocolate mixture into the egg mixture until lightly streaky. Gently fold in the flour mixture. Let the batter rest 5 minutes to thicken.

Using a tablespoon cookie scoop or measuring spoon, drop the batter onto the prepared sheets and bake 9–10 minutes, or until the cookies are puffed and the tops are cracked. Place the baking sheets on wire racks and let cool completely before removing the cookies from the sheets.

When the cookies are cool, melt the caramels and cream in a small nonstick saucepan over low heat, stirring regularly. Stir in the orange oil and let cool slightly. Using a spoon, drizzle the caramel over the cookies. Let set at least 10 minutes.

AUNTIE ANNA'S SUGAR COOKIES
with Orange Frosting

My aunt Anna (who would be 103 now) always made these cookies for the holidays. It is what I most looked forward to at Christmas. She never had a recipe, but right before she passed away, I sat down with her and we worked out this recipe. The combination of nutmeg and sour cream in the cookie dough, along with the orange frosting, was the best. I have given them as gifts for the past thirty years now.

CONTESTANT: DONNA SPEIRS
KENNEBUNK, ME

Cookie Dough

- 4 cups all-purpose flour
- 1 teaspoon baking powder
- ½ teaspoon baking soda
- ½ teaspoon salt
- ½ teaspoon ground nutmeg
- 1 cup butter, softened
- 1½ cups granulated sugar
- 1 egg
- ½ cup sour cream
- 1 teaspoon vanilla extract

Frosting

- 12 tablespoons unsalted butter, softened
- 1 pound confectioners' sugar, sifted
- Zest of 1 orange
- Fresh squeezed juice from 1 orange

Make the cookie dough. Sift the flour with the baking powder, baking soda, salt, and nutmeg. Set aside.

With an electric mixer or stand mixer, beat the butter, sugar, and egg on low speed until light and fluffy. Beat in the sour cream and vanilla until smooth. Gradually add the flour mixture, beating until well combined. With a spatula, form the dough into a ball. Wrap in plastic wrap or waxed paper and refrigerate for at least 1 hour.

Preheat the oven to 375°F.

Divide the dough into four parts. Keep each part refrigerated until you're ready to roll it out. Lightly grease baking sheets, or line them with parchment paper or silicone baking mats. On a well-floured surface, roll the dough, one part at a time, to ¼ inch thick. With a floured cookie cutter, cut the cookies. Place 2–3 inches apart on baking sheets. Bake 10–12 minutes or until golden. Remove to a wire rack to cool.

Make the frosting. Cream the butter with an electric mixer or stand mixer. Add the confectioners' sugar, orange zest, and orange juice and mix to combine. Frost the cookies and decorate with your favorite sprinkles, chopped nuts, and so on.

LINZER COOKIES
(Linzer Plaetzchen)

This is an authentic Austrian/German cookie, based on the classic Viennese linzertorte. This cookie version features raspberry jam topped by pastry latticework. My husband is German, and we lived there for nearly twenty years. Our two boys were both born theret as well. My German mother-in-law passed this cookie recipe down to me, and I cherish it.

CONTESTANT: BRENDA KURCZEWSKI
MOON TOWNSHIP, PA

¾ cup unsalted butter, softened

½ cup granulated sugar

2 jumbo eggs, divided use

1 package vanilla sugar

1 teaspoon Madagascar vanilla extract

1 teaspoon lemon zest

2 cups unsifted all-purpose flour

1 cup ground hazelnuts or natural almonds (or a combination)

¼ teaspoon salt

¼ teaspoon high-quality cocoa powder

½ teaspoon ground cinnamon

¼ teaspoon allspice

4 teaspoons raspberry Schnapps

Raspberry jam for filling

Confectioners' sugar for dusting

Preheat the oven to 375°F. Line baking sheets with parchment paper or silicone baking mats.

In a large bowl, beat the butter until creamy, then gradually mix in the sugar until fluffy. Beat in 1 egg, the vanilla sugar, the vanilla extract, and the lemon zest.

Gradually beat in the flour, ground nuts, salt, cocoa powder, cinnamon, allspice, and raspberry Schnapps, scraping the bowl occasionally, until the dough is well combined. Wrap the dough in foil and refrigerate overnight.

Remove small chunks of the dough at a time and roll thin. Cut with small round cookie cutters. Place on prepared baking sheets. Spread a small amount of raspberry jam onto unbaked rounds (not quite to the edge).

Roll out additional dough and, using a ruler and a pastry wheel, cut small narrow strips. Weave four strips for lattice effect on top of the jam rounds (two in each direction).

Beat the remaining egg in a small bowl. Brush the tops with egg wash and bake for 14–16 minutes or until firm and golden brown.

Cool completely on a wire rack. Sift confectioners' sugar over the tops. Store in airtight containers in the freezer with waxed paper between layers.

Note that the quantity will depend on the thickness of the rolled dough and the diameter of the cookie cutter.

CINNAMON HONEY
Cookies

I get stressed out a lot, usually about big assignments for school or about music gigs. One day, I had the urge to do something constructive with my stress. I looked up a simple cinnamon cookie recipe online and now, after two years of trying different things, I've adapted it. Extra vanilla and the addition of locally harvested honey have transformed the cookies from their dry past to chewy deliciousness. Experimenting with the size of the dough balls has yielded the best possible size and time ratio.

CONTESTANT: MICHELLE TRANTHAM
SPRINGFIELD, MO

1 cup granulated sugar

½ cup salted butter + additional for greasing baking sheets

1 large egg

1 tablespoon vanilla extract

1 tablespoon honey (approximate)

1½ cups all-purpose flour

1½ teaspoons ground cinnamon

1 teaspoon baking powder

Cinnamon/sugar mix (5 parts cinnamon, 7 parts granulated sugar)

In a bowl, mix the sugar and butter until smooth. Beat in the egg, vanilla, and honey. Combine the flour, cinnamon, and baking powder in a separate bowl. Add the dry ingredients to the wet ingredients and blend well. Cover the dough and freeze for 20 minutes, or until firm enough to roll.

Preheat the oven to 350°F. Shape the dough into small spheres about 1 inch in diameter. Roll in the cinnamon/sugar mix to coat. Set the balls 1 inch apart on lightly butter-greased (or nonstick) baking sheets. Bake for 11 minutes or until golden brown. Let cool and enjoy.

MARME'S BEST SUGAR
Cookies

My marme (what we call our grandmother) made a version of these cookies every winter when I was younger, and she would always serve them with mugs of hot cocoa. As I've grown older I've continued to make them every year for my own family, but have tinkered with the recipe a bit to make it perfectly fluffy and buttery. My husband suggested cutting back on the sugar and adding honey to make them more chewy than crispy, so that's the way I've made them the past few years. It may be a simple humble cookie, but no more tinkering is needed.

CONTESTANT: ELIZABETH ICKES

MONROE, MI

3 cups all-purpose flour + additional for rolling

2 teaspoons baking powder

1 teaspoon salt

⅔ cup unsalted butter, softened

1 cup granulated sugar

¼ cup honey

2 large eggs

1 teaspoon vanilla extract

1 tablespoon milk

Sanding sugar for decoration (granulated sugar can be substituted)

Preheat the oven to 375°F.

In a medium bowl, combine the flour, baking powder, and salt. Set aside.

In a large bowl, beat the butter until smooth. Add the sugar and honey, and mix until combined. Add the eggs, one at a time, to the butter mixture and mix together. Add the vanilla and milk and mix again. Add the dry ingredients to the butter mixture and stir until completely combined.

Turn the dough out onto a well-floured table or counter. Press the dough down some with your hand and dust the top with more flour. Roll the dough out with a rolling pin to ½ inch thick. Using cookie cutters, cut out cookie shapes and place onto baking sheets, 1 inch apart. Sprinkle with sanding (or granulated) sugar before baking.

Bake for 8–12 minutes or until the edges are just starting to look golden brown. Cool on a wire rack or enjoy warm.

SPRINKLE
Cookies

I love the big sprinkle cookies that one can find all over New York City, and I thought that it would be fun to make a version of my own.

CONTESTANT: ERINN JOHNSON
MORRISVILLE, PA

1¼ cups all-purpose flour

1 teaspoon cream of tartar

½ teaspoon baking soda

¼ cup unsalted butter, room temperature

¼ cup vegetable shortening, room temperature

¾ cup granulated sugar

1 large egg

¾ cup rainbow sprinkles

Preheat the oven to 350°F. Line two baking sheets with parchment paper or silicone baking mats.

Mix the flour, cream of tartar, and baking soda in a bowl. Set aside.

Combine the butter and shortening in the bowl of an electric mixer or stand mixer fitted with the paddle attachment. Mix on medium speed until light and creamy. Add the sugar and continue to mix until well combined. Add the egg and mix. Scrape the sides of the bowl and mix again.

Add the flour mixture and mix until just combined. Remove the bowl from the mixer and add the rainbow sprinkles. Mix in by hand.

Roll the dough into 15 balls (about 1.4 ounces each). Place on the prepared baking sheets, about 3 inches apart.

Place in the oven and bake for about 14–16 minutes, rotating the sheets halfway through, or until very light brown around the outside edge. You do not want much color on the cookie.

Remove from the oven and transfer the cookies to wire racks to cool.

TRIPLE GINGER AND CRANBERRY
Chewy Biscotti

When in Hawaii more than twenty years ago, I had my first taste of macadamia nuts. When I returned home I used them in many recipes I had been making for years. I learned how to make biscotti from my Italian exchange student in the 1980s.

Biscotti in Italian means "twice baked. All biscotti cookies do not need to be hard and crunchy. In my version, the cookie is slightly chewy.

CONTESTANT: MICHAELA ROSENTHAL
WOODLAND HILLS, CA

⅓ cup canola oil

¼ cup dark molasses

1 cup granulated sugar + additional for rolling the dough

1 egg

1 teaspoon freshly grated ginger

2 cups flour

1 teaspoon baking soda

1 teaspoon ground cloves

¾ teaspoon ground cinnamon

½ teaspoon ground ginger

¼ teaspoon nutmeg

½ teaspoon salt

1 cup chopped macadamia nuts

¾ cup dried (moist) cranberries

¼ cup minced candied ginger

Preheat the oven to 350°F. Line a baking sheet with parchment paper or a silicone baking mat.

Beat together the oil, molasses, sugar, egg, and fresh ginger. In a separate bowl, sift together the flour, baking soda, cloves, cinnamon, ground ginger, nutmeg, and salt. Stir the dry ingredients into the wet. Add nuts, cranberries, and candied ginger and stir until incorporated.

Divide the dough in half and shape each half into a log (approximately 12 × 2 inches). Roll each half in sugar and press to flatten slightly.

Place both logs onto prepared baking sheet and bake for 15 minutes. Remove from the oven and let rest for 5 minutes. Slice (on a diagonal) into ¾ inch slices and separate slightly. Return to the oven and bake an additional 15 minutes. Remove from the oven and transfer to a wire rack to cool.

MEXICAN SNOWFLAKE
Cookies

I taught myself how to bake and cook as a latchkey kid. My mother-in-law, who is from the Midwest, taught me how to bake everything from scratch with an Amish flair. My heritage is Mexican and German, so basically I think it's good to have a little bit of heat in your food. I grew up with Mexican pan dulce treats shaped like little piggies called marranitos, *which were usually eaten with Mexican hot chocolate. I remember my mom bringing home heart-shaped gingerbread cookies on Valentine's Day. They had a hard white candy icing on top. Collecting various recipes from my youth, I have created my own version of this cookie. Instead of pigs or hearts, I like to make snowflakes.*

CONTESTANT: KATHRYN UNDERWOOD
OLYMPIA, WA

Cookie Dough

- 1 cup packed dark brown cane sugar
- 1 cup unsalted butter, room temperature
- 2 large eggs, room temperature
- 1 cup unsulfured molasses
- 4 teaspoons ground cinnamon
- 4 teaspoons powdered ginger
- 1½ teaspoons ground cloves
- 2 teaspoons fine ground black pepper
- ¼ teaspoon powdered red cayenne pepper
- 6 cups all-purpose flour
- 1 teaspoon baking soda
- ½ teaspoon baking powder
- 1 teaspoon sea salt

Royal Icing

- 2 large egg whites
- 4 cups confectioners' sugar, sifted, + additional for cutting out the cookies

  Juice from one lemon

  Blue sugar sprinkles

  Silver dragées

Make the cookie dough. Mix the brown sugar and butter with an electric mixer or stand mixer fitted with the paddle attachment until fluffy, about 5 minutes. Add the eggs, one at a time on low speed, until thoroughly incorporated. Add the molasses at low speed and mix well, scraping down the sides of the bowl after 1 minute. Mix an additional 1 minute.

In a separate small bowl, combine the cinnamon, ginger, cloves, black pepper, and red cayenne pepper. With the mixer off, add the spice mixture to the sugar mixture. Mix on medium-low speed until well mixed. Do not overbeat. Turn off the mixer and set aside.

Sift the all-purpose flour into a separate large bowl. Add the baking soda, baking powder, and salt to the flour mixture and stir gently with a wire whisk.

With the mixer on medium-low speed or by hand with a wooden spoon, slowly add the flour mixture ¼ cup at a time to the wet ingredients until well mixed. Be sure to scrape down the sides of the bowl periodically. Mix well.

Form the dough into a large, long log shape. Cover with plastic wrap and refrigerate for 1 hour.

Make the royal icing while the dough is chilling. Beat the egg whites with the mixer on high speed until the whites are stiff but no dry peaks form.

Slowly add half of the confectioners' sugar, and alternate with half of the lemon juice. Repeat with the rest of the confectioners' sugar and lemon juice.

After dough has chilled, place a sharp knife in a tall glass of hot water. Using the hot knife, divide dough log in half crosswise, then cut each half in half crosswise again. Score and section each of the four pieces into fifths. This should make 20 cookies.

Preheat the oven to 325°F. Stagger pieces of the cookie dough onto a baking sheet lined with parchment paper or a silicone baking mat. Place a 6 × 6 inch piece of plastic wrap over a cookie and flatten with a small rolling pin or the palm of your hand until wide enough to cut out a full shape. Remove the plastic wrap and repeat with the next cookie. Work as quickly as possible. Use a circle or small snowflake cookie cutter dipped into confectioners' sugar to create the shape for each cookie. Using your fingers or a sharp knife, carefully remove the excess dough from around each cookie. Place the excess dough in the refrigerator before rerolling.

Bake cookies for 10–12 minutes. When cool, decorate with royal icing using a pastry bag and blue sugar sprinkles and silver dragées.

FRIESIAN TEA
Cookies

This recipe comes from my father's mother, who was from Friesland in northern Germany. Friesland is so flat that you can see on Friday who is coming to visit for tea on Sunday. This way, the cookies have time to soften in the tin before they are served.

CONTESTANT: SUSANN PINTER
CARBONDALE, IL

1 cup all-purpose flour + additional for rolling

1¼–1½ cups ground almonds (unblanched)

½ cup granulated sugar

1 teaspoon baking powder

⅔ cup butter or margarine, softened

1 egg

½ teaspoon vanilla extract

½ teaspoon almond extract

½ cup red currant jelly

2 tablespoons warm water

In a large bowl, mix all dry ingredients and make a dent in the middle. Put the butter or margarine, egg, and vanilla and almond extracts into the dent. Knead the ingredients until the dough is smooth. Form the dough into a ball and let it rest in the refrigerator for several hours or overnight.

Preheat the oven to 350°F. Sprinkle flour onto a smooth surface. With a rolling pin, roll out half of the dough to a thickness of approximately ¼ inch. Using a cookie cutter, cut out 32 cookies and transfer them to a baking stone (or greased baking sheet). Now cut a peephole into each cookie using a smaller cookie cutter. Bake the cookies for 14 minutes or until lightly browned. Repeat with the remaining dough for the bottom halves of the cookies, but do not cut holes in these.

Cool the cookies on a wire rack. Mix the red currant jelly with warm water until smooth. Put a dab of the jelly mixture onto each bottom cookie piece, and then add a cookie top. Repeat until all the cookies are complete.

It is important to store the cookies in a tin for at least a day or two until the currant jelly moistens and softens the cookie. Enjoy with tea or coffee.

NIGELLA BITES

Back home in Bangladesh we used to have savory cookies with tea. It would have a soft buttery smell and was extremely delicious. I have been living in Arkansas for three years and really miss my favorite flavors. So I came up with my very own version of nigella bites.

CONTESTANT: BIPASHA AHMED
FAYETTEVILLE, AR

⅓ cup + 3 tablespoons butter, room temperature

4 tablespoons confectioners' sugar

1 teaspoon salt

6 tablespoons water

3 pieces cardamom, ground

½ teaspoon nigella seed

¾ teaspoon baking powder

2 cups all-purpose flour + additional for rolling

Clarified butter (optional)

Preheat the oven to 370°F. Using an electric mixer or stand mixer, mix the butter, sugar, and salt. Add the water, cardamom, and nigella to the mixture and beat for 30 seconds. Add the baking powder and flour to the mixture. Make sure to knead for a few minutes. Put a little flour down on a flat surface and on the rolling pin.

Roll out a medium-thick layer of the dough (at least ½ inch). Otherwise it won't be moist and will break apart. Cut the dough with a round cookie cutter. Use a fork to mark holes in the middle of the cookies. For more buttery result, brush clarified butter on top of the cookies. Bake for 15–18 minutes.

Grandma Theresa's
ITALIAN RICOTTA COOKIES

My grandma was born in Calabria and was a wonderful cook. Gram and Grandpa didn't have much money, so for Christmas they would give each of us (grandchildren) these homemade cookies, a five-dollar bill, and lots and lots of unconditional love!

CONTESTANT: DONNA BELLOMO
DUMONT, NJ

Cookie Dough

- ½ cup butter, softened
- 1 cup granulated sugar
- 2 eggs
- 1 teaspoon vanilla extract
- 8 ounces ricotta cheese
- 2 cups all-purpose flour
- ½ teaspoon baking soda
- ¼ teaspoon salt

Frosting

- 2 tablespoons butter, softened
- 2 cups confectioners' sugar
- ¼ teaspoon vanilla extract
- 1½ tablespoons milk

Preheat the oven to 350°F. Line baking sheets with parchment paper or silicone baking mats.

Make the cookie dough. In a medium bowl, cream together the butter and sugar until smooth. Beat in the eggs, one at a time, then stir in the vanilla and ricotta cheese.

In a separate bowl, combine the flour, baking soda, and salt. Gradually stir the flour mixture into the cheese mixture. Drop by rounded teaspoonfuls 2 inches apart onto the prepared baking sheets.

Bake for 8–10 minutes or until the edges are golden. Allow the cookies to cool on the baking sheet for 5 minutes before removing to a wire rack to cool completely.

Make the frosting. In a medium bowl, cream together the butter and confectioners' sugar. Gradually beat in the vanilla and milk until a spreadable consistency is reached. Frost the cooled cookies.

White-Chocolate Stuffed
CRANBERRY GINGERBREAD COOKIES

As a child, I remember walking into my Polish gramma's house during the holidays and smelling the spicy aroma of her gingerbread cookies. I never did receive any of my gramma's recipes, as they were lost with her when she passed away. It has been my passion and determination to create such amazing baked goods as she did. It has taken me some time to master a gingerbread cookie I am fond of. Adding the tart dried cranberries and baking white chocolate in the centers updates this old-fashioned favorite.

CONTESTANT: JULIANA EVANS
ORLANDO, FL

56 white chocolate melting wafers
1 cup margarine, softened (must have 80% vegetable oil)
¾ cup packed dark brown sugar
½ cup packed light brown sugar
½ cup instant French vanilla pudding mix (1 box)
¼ cup molasses
2 eggs
2 teaspoons ground ginger
2 teaspoons ground cinnamon
2 teaspoons pure vanilla extract
1 teaspoon baking soda
1 teaspoon salt
2¼ cups all-purpose flour
1½ cups dried cranberries
Confectioners' sugar for dusting

Preheat the oven to 375°F.

Place the white chocolate wafers in the freezer at least 10 minutes prior to baking. With an electric mixer or stand mixer, beat the margarine until smooth. Add both sugars, then the dry pudding mix. Mix in the molasses, followed by the eggs. Stir in the ginger, cinnamon, and vanilla extract. Add the baking soda and salt. Slowly mix in the flour. On the lowest setting, mix in the dried cranberries.

Scoop out 1 tablespoon dough balls with a scooper; you should get about 56. Set aside. Remove the white chocolate from the freezer.

Place one dough ball in the palm of your hand and flatten. Place two white chocolate discs in the center. Take another dough ball and place it on top of the white chocolate, sandwiching it between the dough pieces. Roll in the palm of your hand to form a ball and place on a baking sheet.

Continue this process, making 6 balls and placing them 2–3 inches apart on baking sheet. Bake for 11 minutes. Continue working on the remaining dough while the other cookies are baking.

Allow to cool slightly until warm in the pan. Remove and sprinkle with confectioners' sugar. Enjoy.

Vegan, Gluten-Free, Paleo
SUGAR COOKIES

When I think of the holidays, I think of cookies. Growing up, we had a tradition of making hundreds of Christmas cookies to share with family and friends. I have many fond memories in the kitchen, stamping out the dough, frosting the cookies, and of course eating the tasty little treats. With our sugar cookie recipe it's okay to indulge a little this holiday season. We wanted to come up with a healthier alternative to the sugar cookie, something everyone could enjoy regardless of dietary restrictions.

CONTESTANT: STEPHANIE WEEKS
WAY ARVADO, CO

Cookie Dough

- 1½ cups confectioners' sugar
- ⅛ teaspoon salt
- 1 cup coconut oil, soft but not melted
- ¼ cup unsweetened coconut milk
- 1 teaspoon vanilla extract
- 2½ cups unbleached all-purpose gluten-free flour
- 2 tablespoons arrowroot powder
- 1 teaspoon baking soda
- 1 teaspoon cream of tartar

Icing

- 2 cups confectioners' sugar
- 2 tablespoons coconut or almond milk
- 1 teaspoon pure almond extract
- Food coloring (optional)

Make the cookie dough. In a large bowl, beat the confectioners' sugar, salt, coconut oil, coconut milk, and vanilla with an electric mixer or stand mixer on medium speed to combine. Sift in the remaining ingredients and beat until blended. If dough is too crumbly, add a splash more coconut milk. Divide the dough in half, cover, and refrigerate at least 1 hour.

Preheat the oven to 375°F. Line a baking sheet with parchment paper or silicone baking mat. If the dough is too stiff, let it warm up a little before rolling it out. On a floured surface, roll each dough half to ¼ inch thick. Use cookie cutters to make your favorite shapes. Place the dough shapes on the baking sheet 2 inches apart and bake 7–8 minutes. Allow the cookies to cool completely on a wire rack before decorating.

Make the icing. Place the confectioners' sugar, coconut or almond milk, and almond extract in a small bowl. Whisk until smooth. Add in a couple drops of food coloring if you like. If the mixture is too runny, add confectioners' sugar until it can easily be spread without running off the cookies. Spread the icing on the cookies.

LEEANNE'S CREAM CHEESE CUT-OUT
Cookies

My aunt used to make these when I was a child. My love for baking began when I was twelve and started with Christmas cookies! Since I have turned it into a Web business, I have taken those recipes and tweaked them a bit to make them mine. This one is a favorite of all my friends and family. I am asked for the recipe every time someone new tries them. I make them for every holiday and use holiday cookie cutters to match whatever the occasion may be. But Christmas is by far the most popular requested time to make these.

CONTESTANT: LEEANNE SNOW
SCHAUMBURG, IL

Cookie Dough

- ½ cup butter, room temperature
- 3 ounces cream cheese
- 2¾ cups all-purpose flour
- 1¼ cups sifted confectioners' sugar or granulated sugar
- 1 egg
- ½ teaspoon baking powder
- ½ teaspoon salt
- 1 teaspoon vanilla extract
- ½ teaspoon almond extract

Icing

- 3 cups sifted confectioners' sugar
- 2 tablespoons butter
- 2 tablespoons cream cheese
- ½ teaspoon vanilla extract
- 1 teaspoon almond extract
- Milk
- Food coloring (optional)
- Sprinkles

Make the cookie dough. Beat the butter and cream cheese with an electric mixer or stand mixer on medium speed. Add about half of the flour, then the sugar, egg, baking powder, salt, and vanilla and almond extracts. Beat on low speed until combined. Beat in the remaining flour on low speed.

Divide the dough in half, cover, and refrigerate for 1 hour. Preheat the oven to 325°F. Line baking sheets with parchment paper or silicone baking mats. Roll out the dough on a lightly floured surface to ¼ inch thick. Cut out shapes with cookie cutters. Arrange on prepared baking sheets. Bake for about 15 minutes or until the edges are light brown. Transfer to a wire rack and cool completely.

Make the icing. Beat together the confectioners' sugar, butter, and cream cheese in a small bowl. Add the vanilla and almond extracts. Stir in milk, 1 teaspoon at a time, until the icing is piping or drizzle consistency. Add food coloring if desired. Decorate the cookies with icing and sprinkles.

BRUNA BROD
(Swedish Butter Cookies)

This recipe came from Sweden when my ancestors moved here around the turn of the twentieth century. My great-aunt Hulda made these cookies, my grammy made them, my mom made them, and now I make them. It's very important to use your hands to make the dough; I'm not sure why, but I think there's magic in your hands that comes out when you make the cookies.

CONTESTANT: LAURA EATON
LEOLA, PA

1 **cup butter, softened**
1 **cup granulated sugar**
1 **tablespoon dark corn syrup**
1 **teaspoon baking soda**
2 **cups flour**

Preheat the oven to 375°F.

Cream together the butter and sugar. Add the corn syrup and blend well. Add the baking soda and flour. Using your hands, mix until a dough forms. Make into a ball, and then divide into four sections.

Line baking sheets with parchment paper or silicone baking mats. Take one-quarter of the dough and form it into a long line the width of your thumb. Place two of these lines of dough on each sheet.

Bake the cookies for 15–20 minutes, waiting until they are golden brown. Using a spatula, cut the strips on an angle, about 12–16 cookies per strip, while the cookies are hot. Let cool on the baking sheet for 2 minutes. Slide the cookies off the sheet and let cool completely on wire racks.

PEKING CARAMEL-GANACHE
Cookies

I got the inspiration for this recipe when I made caramel sauce. To make it interesting, I add three ingredients that are common in Chinese cooking. That's why I call these Peking Caramel-Ganache Cookies.

CONTESTANT: SUGIYARTI JORGENSON
KODIAK, AK

Ganache Filling

- 2 ounces bittersweet chocolate
- ¼ cup heavy cream
- 1 tablespoon confectioners' sugar
- 1 teaspoon ground star anise

Cookie Dough

- 1¼ cups all-purpose flour
- ½ teaspoon baking soda
- ½ cup sesame seeds
- ½ cup granulated sugar
- ¼ cup packed brown sugar
- ½ cup butter
- ¼ teaspoon sea salt
- 1½ teaspoons toasted sesame oil
- ½ teaspoon vanilla extract
- 1 large egg

Make the ganache filling. Combine the chocolate, heavy cream, confectioners' sugar, and star anise in a medium bowl. Microwave on high power for 30 seconds until hot. Stir until smooth; refrigerate for 30 minutes.

Preheat the oven to 375°F. Line baking sheets with parchment paper or silicone baking mats.

Make the cookie dough. Combine the flour and baking soda in a medium bowl; set aside. Spread the sesame seeds on a plate.

Combine the sugars in a medium saucepan; heat over medium-high heat. After the edges start to melt, stir with wooden spoon until completely melted. Lower the heat and add the butter. Stir until the butter is melted. Remove the mixture from the heat and whisk constantly until slightly cooled. Add the salt, sesame oil, vanilla, and egg. Whisk until thick, about 30 seconds. Transfer to a medium bowl; let stand for 3 minutes. Whisk for another 30 seconds. Using a spatula, stir in the flour mixture until well mixed. If necessary, refrigerate the dough for 20 minutes or until it is easy to handle.

Take 2 tablespoons dough; flatten it and fill with 1 teaspoon ganache. Shape into a ball, then roll in sesame seeds. Place the dough ball on the prepared baking sheet. Repeat with the remaining dough. Bake the cookies for 10–12 minutes or until the edges are set. Cool in the pan for 5 minutes, then transfer to a wire rack and cool completely.

CHOC-TAMALES

A few years ago I moved from the Southeast to Southern California and spent the holiday with my Mexican American friend and his family. The joyous times and the wonderful new treats inspired me to make these adorable little tamale cookies. They are heated with cinnamon, chocolate, and chiles, and filled with pecans and cornmeal, which are favorites of both my old and new homes.

CONTESTANT: AUTUMN CLEMENTS

LOS ANGELES, CA

1½ cups all-purpose flour + additional for rolling

½ cup + 3 tablespoons fine-ground cornmeal, divided use

1 teaspoon salt, divided use

8 ounces unsalted butter, softened

6 ounces cream cheese, softened

½ cup granulated sugar

1 cup pecan halves

2 ounces bittersweet chocolate, chopped fine

¾ cup brown sugar

1 teaspoon ground cinnamon

¼ teaspoon ground cayenne pepper

½ teaspoon ground ancho chile powder

½ cup pepper jelly (jalapeño or red)

¼ cup demerara sugar

Dried corn husk for tying (optional)

Chocolate for drizzling (optional)

In a medium bowl, whisk the flour, ½ cup of the cornmeal, and ½ teaspoon of the salt.

In a large bowl, beat the butter and cream cheese with an electric mixer or stand mixer until fluffy, then beat in the granulated sugar. Add the flour mixture half at a time, until just incorporated. Reserve ¾ cup of the dough. Wrap the remaining dough in plastic cling wrap and refrigerate for at least 1 hour.

Preheat the oven to 350°F. Spread the pecans on a baking sheet and toast until fragrant, turning once, about 6–8 minutes. Chop fine. Place in a medium bowl with the chocolate, brown sugar, cinnamon, cayenne, ancho, remaining salt, and reserved dough. Beat until combined to make the filling.

Halve the chilled dough. Roll each half on a lightly floured board into a 6 × 12 inch rectangle. Cut each piece lengthwise into 3 × 12 inch strips, trimming off the ragged edges. Spoon 2 tablespoons of the jelly down the center of each of the four strips.

Divide the filling into four equal portions and form each into a log 12 inches long. Place over the jelly on the chilled dough strips. Bring the long sides up and press to seal the seam. Gently roll each length back and forth to lengthen to 18 inches, then cut each log into six tamales. Sprinkle with demerara sugar and the remaining 3 tablespoons of cornmeal. Press gently to adhere.

Freeze the tamales on parchment or silicone baking mat for 10 minutes. Place the parchment or baking mat on a baking sheet and bake for 15–18 minutes or until set and golden on the bottom. Cool. Tie with small pieces of dried corn husk and/or drizzle with chocolate for presentation.

HEART-OF-SPICE SOFT MOLASSES
Cookies

The original cookie recipe came from a family that I attended church with. I tinkered with the spices and baking times and techniques. I found that an air-insulated pan and cookie scoop created the perfect blend of crisp outside and soft inside.

CONTESTANT: ROCHELLE PIPER
FULDA, MN

2¼ cups granulated sugar, divided use

½ cup vegetable shortening

2 eggs

¾ cup molasses

1 teaspoon vanilla extract

3 cups all-purpose flour

1½ teaspoons ground ginger

1 teaspoon ground cinnamon

¼ teaspoon ground cloves

½ teaspoon cardamom

1 teaspoon dried orange peel

1½ teaspoons baking soda

½ teaspoon salt

Preheat the oven to 375°F.

Beat together 1¼ cup of the sugar and the shortening. Add the eggs, molasses, and vanilla, beating well until smooth, about 1 minute.

In separate bowl, stir together the flour, ginger, cinnamon, cloves, cardamom, orange peel, baking soda, and salt. Add the dry ingredients to the molasses mixture and stir together.

Drop by medium cookie scoop (approximately 2 tablespoons) into a small bowl filled with the remaining 1 cup of sugar. Roll the cookie dough in the sugar to completely cover. Bake on air-insulated baking sheets for 10 minutes. Take out of the oven while cookies are still slightly raised and drop the pan down onto counter. The cookies will crack beautifully.

Note: For extra-large, café-size cookies, use a large cookie scoop or ice cream scoop (approximately ¼ cup) and bake for 15 minutes.

HOLIDAY COOKIE-BUTTER
Cookies

This cookie doesn't have much of a history, because I just created it for my recent obsession with jarred cookie butter. I developed this recipe to present a flavorful spiced cookie base of cardamom, cinnamon, ginger, and cloves. I love the way this festive cookie has something yummy in every bite.

CONTESTANT: LANIE SMITH
TOPEKA, KS

- ½ cup unsalted butter, room temperature
- ⅓ cup butter-flavored vegetable shortening
- ¾ cup granulated sugar
- ½ cup packed dark brown sugar
- 1 egg
- ½ teaspoon sea salt
- ¾ teaspoon baking soda
- 1¼ teaspoons ground cinnamon
- ½ teaspoon ground ginger
- ¼ teaspoon ground cardamom
- ¼ teaspoon ground cloves
- 2 cups all-purpose flour
- 1 cup gingerbread cookie butter spread, stirred well
- 1½ cups white chocolate chips

Preheat the oven to 350°F.

In a large bowl, beat the butter and shortening until smooth, about 1 minute. Add the granulated sugar, brown sugar, egg, salt, and baking soda. Continue mixing for 30 seconds on low speed. Add the cinnamon, ginger, cardamom, and cloves. Mix on low speed until combined. Slowly add in the flour and mix until well incorporated. The dough will be thick.

Wrap the dough in plastic and refrigerate for 20 minutes. Line baking sheets with parchment paper or silicone baking mats.

Roll the dough into balls using ¼ cup of dough for each and place on the prepared baking sheets 4 inches apart. Indent the centers of each ball with a tablespoon, ¾ inch deep. Place 1 heaping teaspoon of cookie butter into each center.

Insert about 8 white chocolate chips around the edges of each cookie with the pointy side of the chip into the dough. Bake for 15–17 minutes until golden brown around the edges. Let the cookies cool completely on the sheet.

MICHELE'S RAINBOW
Cookies

I first discovered these cookies on a trip to New York City. As a lover of marzipan, I couldn't resist these delectable cookies, having first tried them at Ferrara Bakery in Little Italy. It took plenty of trial and error to perfect my recipe but it has always been a labor of love, and today I think my version of Italian rainbow cookies, or Italian tricolor cookies, are the very best of any that I've tasted.

CONTESTANT: MICHELE MARTISE
KIRKWOOD, MO

Cookie Dough

8	ounces pure almond paste
1¼	cups granulated sugar
6	eggs, room temperature
1½	cups unsalted butter, softened
1¼	cups all-purpose flour
1¼	tablespoons pure almond extract
¼	teaspoon salt
	Red food coloring
	Green food coloring
	Cooking spray

Filling

Seedless raspberry or apricot jam

Chocolate Icing

12	ounces semisweet chocolate morsels
1	tablespoon pure vegetable oil

Preheat the oven to 325°F.

Make the cookie dough. Mix together almond paste and sugar. Beat in the eggs, then the butter. Add the flour and mix well. Mix in the almond extract, then the salt.

Divide the dough equally into three bowls. Add 23 drops of red food coloring to one bowl and mix thoroughly. Add 23 drops of green food coloring to another bowl and mix thoroughly. Leave the last bowl of dough as is (no food coloring).

Spray three shallow 9 × 9 baking sheets with cooking spray. Spread the red dough in one pan, the green dough in another, and the plain dough in the last pan. Bake for approximately 15 minutes. Remove from the oven and cool on a wire rack.

Make the filling. Once the cookies are cooled, warm the jam in a small saucepan. Place it onto parchment paper or silicone baking mat. Spread the green layer thinly but evenly with half the jam. Place the plain layer on top of the green layer and spread with the remaining jam. Place the red layer on top. Cut lengthwise into three equal "loaves."

Make the chocolate icing. Pour the chocolate morsels into a small saucepan. Heat just enough to melt the chips, then add the vegetable oil and stir until well combined. Pour the melted chocolate over each section (top and all sides). Place the loaves in the freezer for 30 minutes, until the chocolate coating sets. Once set, wrap each loaf individually in waxed or parchment paper. Wrap each loaf in aluminum foil after that, and return them to the freezer. When ready to serve, unwrap a loaf and cut into 1 inch squares.

OMG COOKIES

They say less is more, but sometimes more is more. I have perfected my chocolate chip cookie recipe over the years, and it has been a favorite among my friends and family. One day, after using random leftovers from my pantry (like half bags of chocolate chips, extra homemade toffee, and a bag of snack-size pretzels), I had almost created this cookie, and it was amazing. Then I stuffed in a salted caramel. The result was OMG, so good.

RUNNER-UP: SANDY AREVALO
CRYSTAL LAKE, IL

1 cup unsalted butter, slightly softened, not room temperature

1 cup brown sugar

¾ cup granulated sugar

1 teaspoon pure vanilla extract

2 eggs

2 cups all-purpose flour

1 cup whole wheat flour

¾ teaspoon salt

¾ teaspoon baking soda

½ teaspoon cinnamon

1 cup semisweet chocolate chunks

1 cup milk chocolate chips

½ cup thin pretzel rods, roughly chopped

½ cup toffee pieces, roughly chopped (I use homemade, but store-bought is fine)

24 salted caramels, unwrapped (I use homemade, but store-bought is fine)

Preheat the oven to 375°F. Line baking sheets with parchment paper or silicone baking mats.

With an electric mixer or a stand mixer fitted with a paddle attachment, combine the butter and sugars together until creamy. Add the vanilla and eggs and beat until fully incorporated.

Gradually add the flours, salt, baking soda, and cinnamon, mixing well to combine.

Stir in the chocolate chunks, chocolate chips, pretzels, and toffee pieces by hand.

Firmly pack the dough into a ¼ cup measure and drop, about 2–3 inches apart, onto the prepared baking sheet.

Press a salted caramel into the center of each cookie and press around the edges to make sure the caramel is completely covered.

Bake for 12 minutes, or until the edges are just turning golden brown and the centers are still soft.

Allow to cool for 10 minutes on the baking sheet before transferring them to a wire rack to cool completely.

ICE CREAM NUT OR APRICOT
Horns

My mother, who was a fabulous baker, taught me how to make these cookies many years ago, and I have continued to do so with my son and daughter. We always make a portion of the batch with nut filling and a portion with apricot filling, but I have also made them with cherry or pineapple filling. These cookies were only made at special times of the year, namely Easter and Christmas. The recipe has been passed on many times. Once people taste the cookie, they are surprised to discover that the dough has only three ingredients.

CONTESTANT: D. MASTERS
PITTSBURGH, PA

Cookie Dough

- 1 pound butter, softened
- 4½ cups all-purpose flour + additional for rolling
- 16 ounces vanilla or chocolate ice cream, softened
- Granulated sugar

Nut Filling

- ½ cup margarine
- 1 cup granulated sugar
- ½ cup milk
- 2 egg yolks
- ½ teaspoon cinnamon
- 2 cups ground walnuts

Apricot Filling

- 2 jars of apricot filling, or any other flavor you prefer

Make the cookie dough. With an electric mixer or stand mixer, combine the butter with the flour, a little at a time. When incorporated, mix in the softened ice cream. Remove the dough from the mixer and add additional flour if needed to form a ball. Divide the dough in half and set aside.

Make the nut filling. Melt the margarine in a saucepan over low heat. Add the sugar, milk, egg yolks, and cinnamon, and stir to incorporate. Add the nuts and simmer over low heat until thick, about 5 minutes. Cool.

Preheat the oven to 350°F. Line baking sheets with parchment paper or silicone baking mats.

Divide one of the dough halves into manageable portions and roll out thin on a surface lightly dusted with a mixture of flour and granulated sugar. Cut the dough into squares with a fancy cutter. Drop nut filling in the center of each square and roll in the shape of a horn. Place cookies on the baking sheet and sprinkle with additional granulated sugar.

Repeat with the remaining nut filling for the rest of that half of the dough. Then repeat the process with the apricot filling and the other dough half. Bake for 20–25 minutes, until browned on the bottoms.

GRAM'S CINNAMON NUT ROLL-UP
Cookies

I have warm memories of Gram's kitchen. Every Christmas, the smell of freshly baked cookies dusted in cinnamon spread throughout the house. One regret I had after Gram passed away in 2000 was that I never baked her "famous" cookies with her. Worse yet, no one had the recipe…or at least that's what we thought. Back in 2009, I finally discovered the recipe. I've been making the cookies every Christmas since, and although they don't taste just like hers, they're just as amazing as I remembered.

CONTESTANT: AMY BUCKELEW
BRIDGEWATER, NJ

4 cups all-purpose flour + additional for rolling

1½ cups butter, softened

4 teaspoons baking powder

1 teaspoon salt

2 eggs

1 cup milk

1 teaspoon vanilla extract

1½ cups walnuts, finely chopped

1½ cups granulated sugar

3 teaspoons cinnamon

Powdered sugar for dusting

Combine the flour, butter, baking powder, salt, eggs, milk, and vanilla. Mix the dough by hand. Refrigerate for 3 hours. Divide the dough into 10 equal-sized balls, cover with a wet dishtowel, and refrigerate overnight.

Preheat the oven to 325°F. Line baking sheets with parchment paper or silicone baking mats.

Combine the walnuts, sugar, and cinnamon. Take only one ball out of the refrigerator at a time. Roll each ball out on a floured surface, pressing one tenth of the nut mixture into the dough as you roll. Roll the ball into a circle about ⅛ inch thick. Cut into 10–12 wedges (I use a pizza cutter). Roll each wedge into a crescent shape and place on the prepared baking sheet.

Bake about 25 minutes until golden brown. Cool completely, then sprinkle with powdered sugar.

CARROT CAKE UNSCOTTI

Years before I started teaching, I worked in corporate America and would save vacation time so I could take off for almost two weeks at the end of the year to make cookies. I had requests from the supervisors at the company I worked for to purchase cookie trays or gift baskets for gifts, but I no longer had the time to spend making cookies. I make other unscotti cookies and realized that my carrot cake cookies were one of the most popular, so why not try to make that an easier cookie.

CONTESTANT: DONNA DONOHUE
EXTON, PA

Cookie Dough

- 4 cups all-purpose flour
- 3 teaspoons baking powder
- 2 tablespoons ground cinnamon
- 1 cup butter, softened
- 1½ cups granulated sugar
- 2 tablespoons brown sugar
- 2 teaspoons vanilla extract
- ½ teaspoon salt
- 4 eggs
- 1½ cups walnuts, chopped
- 1 cup carrots, shredded (wrap in a paper towel to dry slightly)
- 1⅓ cups golden raisins (can substitute regular raisins)

Drizzle

- 1½ tablespoons butter, melted
- 1½ cups confectioners' sugar
- ⅛ teaspoon ground cinnamon
- 1 teaspoon vanilla extract
- ⅛ teaspoon salt
- 2–3 tablespoons milk

Make the cookie dough. Whisk together the flour, baking powder, and cinnamon in a bowl; set aside. Beat the butter, sugars, vanilla, and salt until well blended. Beat the eggs into the butter mixture one at a time. Slowly add the flour mixture and beat on low speed. Stir in by hand the walnuts, carrots, and raisins.

Separate the batter into two parts for large unscotti or four for small unscotti. On a piece of parchment or waxed paper, form each portion of batter into a loaf (about 12–13 inches long by 3 inches wide for large, or about 9 inches long by 1½–2 inches wide for small). Wrap each loaf in the parchment paper. Place the wrapped loaves onto a baking sheet and refrigerate to set up for a minimum of 2 hours (up to 4 days).

Preheat the oven to 350°F. Bake the loaves on a parchment-lined baking sheet or pizza stone for 40 minutes. Remove from the oven. Leave the unscotti loaves on the sheets for at least 20 minutes before trying to move to a wire rack. Leave on the wire rack for about 25 minutes before cutting into strips about ¾ inch wide.

Make the drizzle. While the loaves are cooling, combine the butter, confectioners' sugar, cinnamon, vanilla, and salt for the drizzle. Add the milk slowly, using just enough to get the right consistency for drizzling. Use a fork or a cake decorating squeeze bottle to drizzle the cooled cookie strips. Allow the drizzle to set up before packing the cookies in an airtight container.

Salty, Sweet, and Tart
FANTASY TRAIL COOKIES

My original recipe was inspired by a popular trail mix granola bar. My ultimate trail mix creation takes a classic light and crispy vanilla-kissed sugar cookie and crowns it with a sweet, salty, and tart fruit-and-nut mixture coated with a rich brown sugar and honey glaze. All this goodness is topped with a touch of semisweet chocolate.

CONTESTANT: LIDDIA HADDADIAN
PASADENA, CA

Cookie Dough

- 3 cups + 2 tablespoons all-purpose flour, divided use
- 1 teaspoon baking powder
- ¼ teaspoon salt
- 1 cup butter, room temperature
- ½ cup granulated sugar
- ½ cup packed brown sugar
- 1 egg, room temperature
- 1½ teaspoons vanilla extract

Topping

- 1½ cups dried cherries
- 1 cup salted and roasted cashews, coarsely chopped
- 1 cup honey-roasted peanuts
- 1 cup raw sunflower seeds
- ¾ cup water
- 6 tablespoons unsalted butter
- 1½ cups light brown sugar
- 4½ tablespoons honey
- 1½ teaspoons vanilla extract
- 1 cup semisweet chocolate chips (or chunks)
- 1 teaspoon shortening

Make the cookie dough. In a medium bowl, combine 3 cups of the flour, baking powder, and salt. Set aside.

In a large bowl, cream the butter and sugars until creamy (about 3–5 minutes); mix in the egg and vanilla. Add the flour mixture (1 cup at a time) to the creamed mixture, mixing after each addition. Once the dough is well combined, cover with plastic wrap and refrigerate for at least 2 hours or overnight.

Preheat the oven to 375°F. Line two baking sheets with parchment paper or silicone baking mats.

On a lightly floured surface, roll the dough to about ¼ inch thick. Using a fluted 3-inch cookie cutter, cut out 30 cookies. Place on the prepared baking sheets and refrigerate for about 15 minutes.

Make the topping. In a large glass bowl, combine the dried cherries, cashews, peanuts, and sunflower seeds. Set aside. In a medium saucepan over high heat, bring the water, butter, brown sugar, honey, and vanilla to a boil. Lower heat to medium and simmer until the mixture becomes syrupy, mixing every 2 minutes (about 15 minutes total cooking time). Pour the hot mixture over the cherry mixture and mix until well coated.

Top each cookie with one heaping tablespoon of the topping mixture. Bake for 10 minutes. Remove from the oven and cool for a few minutes, then move to a wire rack.

Melt the chocolate and shortening in the microwave until smooth and creamy. Place in a plastic piping bag and cut very small end (or use a tiny round decorating tip). Pipe a thin line of melted chocolate over cookie in a zigzag pattern. Allow the cookies to cool completely before serving. Enjoy!

My Nanny's
CUCCIDATE-MILLIE GIGLIO

So much work goes into these cookies, and I remember as a child my grandmother did all this by hand. She always kept her big rolling pin and the wooden board she used for baking in the hall closet in a pillowcase. To this day I do the same. Thank you, Nanny, for all those hours upon hours of baking, and thank God I remember all your baking items. They stay alive in my mind and always in my heart.

CONTESTANT: PAULA GATI
MILLER PLACE, NY

Cookie Dough

- 4 cups all-purpose flour + additional for kneading
- ½ cup sugar
- 1½ teaspoons baking powder
- ½ teaspoon salt
- 1½ cups butter, cut in ½ inch cubes
- ¼ cup shortening, cold and broken into small pieces
- 2 eggs
- ½ cup milk
- 2 teaspoons vanilla extract

Filling

- 12 ounces dried figs
- ½ cup pitted dates
- ½ cup raisins
- ½ cup almonds, chopped, not too fine
- ⅓ cup honey
- ¼ cup orange marmalade
- ¼ cup whiskey
- 1 teaspoon ground cinnamon

Icing

- 4 cups confectioners' sugar
- A few tablespoons milk
- Nonpareils for decorating

Make the cookie dough. With an electric mixer or stand mixer, mix the flour, sugar, baking powder, and salt. Add the butter pieces a few at a time to the mixture, then the cold shortening.

In a separate bowl, mix the eggs, milk, and vanilla. Slowly add the wet mixture to the dry mixture until a dough forms. Knead the dough a few minutes until it is smooth, adding more flour if necessary. Make a smooth ball, cover it in plastic wrap, and refrigerate it while you prepare the filling.

Make the filling. Remove the stems from the figs. Put the figs, dates, and raisins through a meat grinder or food processor. When all the fruit is ground up, add the remaining ingredients and mix really well. Let sit overnight for all the flavors to really marry.

Preheat the oven to 350°F. Line baking sheets with parchment paper or silicone baking mats.

Start the assembly by taking one quarter of the dough at a time and rolling it out to make a 3 × 12 inch rectangle. Cut the edges with a knife to square off. Take one quarter of the filling and make a log 12 inches long. Place this log onto the rectangle of dough and roll, ending with the seam side down. Cut into approximately 1½ inch pieces and place on the baking sheet. Bake approximately 15 minutes, until the bottoms are slightly golden.

Make the icing. Mix the confectioners' sugar with milk to your desired consistency.

After the cookies are cool, spread a little icing onto each little bundle and sprinkle with some nonpareils.

ANYTHING CAN HAPPEN THURSDAY
Cookies

I am part of a group of four girlfriends called the "Cookie Beotches." Every year, the Thursday after Thanksgiving, I host a cookie-baking marathon. This year, we made a recipe called snowball cookies. While making them, we talked about how we could reinvent the cookies to include our two favorite ingredients: chocolate and coffee. We played around with the snowball cookies recipe and came up with this variation. The name comes from my favorite TV show, The Big Bang Theory. *The characters have what's called "Anything Can Happen Thursday," where they do not do their usual activity for the day. So we decided to call this cookie Anything Can Happen Thursday Cookies—appropriately so, since our baking day is always on a Thursday.*

CONTESTANT: NICOLE JANSSENS
MILLTOWN, NJ

1 cup unsalted butter, softened

1 teaspoon instant espresso powder

½ cup confectioners' sugar + additional for dusting

2 cups all-purpose flour

¼ cup dark cocoa

¼ teaspoon salt

¼ cup boiling water

2 cups flaked coconut + additional for rolling

Preheat the oven to 350°F.

In a large bowl, cream together the butter, espresso powder, and confectioners' sugar until light and fluffy.

In a separate bowl, combine the flour, cocoa, and salt. Add the boiling water and stir. Gradually add the flour mixture to the creamed mixture and mix well. Stir in the coconut. Shape into 1 inch balls and roll in additional coconut.

Place on ungreased baking sheets 2 inches apart. Bake for 10–13 minutes. Cool on the pan for 3 minutes before removing to a wire rack. Dust with additional confectioners' sugar.

ORANGE BLOSSOM MADELEINE COOKIES
with Pomegranate Glaze

These madeleine cookies make my heart sing. Though they may appear deceptively naïve in their simplicity, one bite and you'll be the wiser. I am always in search of fresh, seasonal bounties and revel in explorations of global flavors. The moment my eye caught the inviting garnet hues of a heap of stunning pomegranates against a backdrop of Cara Cara oranges at the produce market, my dad instantly came to mind, as these were his most favorite fruits. Though it has been many years since my father's passing, I still remember fondly his affinity for pastry and his love of my baking, which I took such pride in. I would like to think he'd have loved these cookies, and I hope you will, too.

CONTESTANT: EFFIE SAHIHI
HENDERSONVILLE, TN

Cookie Dough

- 14 tablespoons unsalted butter, melted and cooled, divided use
- 1 cup all-purpose flour + additional for dusting the pans
- 2 eggs, room temperature
- ¼ teaspoon fine sea salt
- ½ cup granulated sugar
- ½ teaspoon ground cardamom
- 2 tablespoons orange zest
- ½ teaspoon orange blossom water

Pomegranate Glaze

- ¾ cup confectioners' sugar
- 3 tablespoons pomegranate juice
- Pinch of fine sea salt

Prepare two madeleine pans by brushing the molds with 4 tablespoons of the melted butter. Dust the pans with flour, then flip the pans over and tap to remove the excess flour. Place the pans in the freezer while you prepare the dough.

Make the cookie dough. Whisk the eggs and salt with an electric mixer or a stand mixer on medium-high speed until the mixture has increased in volume and become pale yellow in color, about 5 minutes. Reduce the mixer to medium-low speed and gradually begin adding the sugar until it's incorporated. Continue beating the egg mixture until it is even paler in color, thick, and creamy, with ribbons forming in the bowl when the whisk is lifted. This will take another 5–7 minutes.

Sift the flour and cardamom directly into the egg mixture and fold it into the batter until just mixed. Fold in the orange zest until just combined. Stir the orange blossom water into the remaining 10 tablespoons of butter, then drizzle into the batter a few tablespoons at a time.

Cover the bowl with plastic wrap and refrigerate for at least 1 hour.

Make the pomegranate glaze. Whisk the confectioners' sugar, pomegranate juice, and salt together in a small bowl until the mixture is completely smooth. Set aside.

Preheat the oven to 375°F. Fill each mold in the madeleine pans with batter to approximately two-thirds of the way full. Do not spread the batter. Bake until they are a light golden brown and spring back slightly when touched, approximately 14–16 minutes. Allow the madeleine cookies to cool in the pan for 1 minute. Carefully loosen the edges with a small spatula or butter knife and then gently release onto a wire rack, with the scalloped side facing up. Immediately toss each madeleine in the pomegranate glaze, turning over several times to coat well, then shake off the excess glaze and set on the wire rack with the scalloped side facing up. Allow the glaze to dry for 15 minutes, then serve. The cookies may be stored in a sealed container for up to 3 days, though they are best eaten the same day.

CHEWY SPECIAL
Cookies

When I was a child, my mom would bake peanut butter blossom cookies around the holidays. Anytime she would bake these cookies, I would eagerly volunteer to be her baking assistant. My favorite part was putting the chocolate kiss in the center of the baked peanut butter cookie rolled in sugar. This is a fond memory that I have with my mom. As an adult, I have continued this love for baking and making these cookies.

CONTESTANT: LAURA GILBERT
PORTLAND, OR

1¼ cups all-purpose flour
¾ teaspoon baking soda
½ teaspoon baking powder
¼ teaspoon salt
½ cup unsalted butter, softened
1 cup crunchy peanut butter
¾ cup granulated sugar
½ cup brown sugar
1 egg
1 tablespoon milk
1 teaspoon vanilla extract
1½ cups chopped Snickers candy bars (about 4 regular size bars)
¼ cup dark chocolate chips
¼ cup white chocolate chips

Preheat the oven to 350°F. Line two baking sheets with parchment paper or silicone baking mats. Set aside.

In a medium bowl, whisk together the flour, baking soda, baking powder, and salt. Set aside.

With an electric mixer or stand mixer, beat the butter and peanut butter together until fluffy. Add the sugars and beat until smooth. Add the egg and mix until combined. Add the milk and the vanilla and mix again. Add the flour mixture and beat until the flour disappears. Stir in the chopped Snickers bars and chocolate chips.

Drop by heaping tablespoons onto the prepared baking sheets. (I weighed mine out to about 2 ounces of dough per cookie.) Gently flatten each cookie ball with the palm of your hand. Bake for 10–11 minutes, or until the cookies are slightly brown on the edges.

Cool the cookies on the baking sheets for about 5–10 minutes, then remove to a wire rack to cool completely. Store in an airtight container at room temperature.

TROPICAL FLORENTINES
with Pineapple Coconut Filling

I created this recipe because I eat gluten-free, and florentines happen to be a great gluten-free cookie. By making them a sandwich cookie, layered with sweet filling, I was able to make them more exciting.

CONTESTANT: SONYA GOERGEN
MOORHEAD, MN

1 8.75-ounce can mixed nuts with macadamia nuts (gluten-free)

3 tablespoons regular or gluten-free flour (use a mix that contains xanthan gum)

Zest of one lime

2 tablespoons heavy cream

2 tablespoons honey

5 tablespoons + ¼ cup butter, divided use

¾ cup granulated sugar

½ teaspoon vanilla extract

2 cups confectioners' sugar

1–2 tablespoons pineapple juice

4 tablespoons finely chopped pineapple (if using canned crushed, drain really well)

4 tablespoons coconut flakes

Preheat the oven to 350°F. Line baking sheets with parchment paper or silicone baking mats.

Pulse the nuts in a food processor until finely chopped. Place the nuts in a bowl and combine with the flour and lime zest. Set aside.

In a medium saucepan over high heat, combine the heavy cream, honey, 5 tablespoons of the butter, and sugar. Bring to a boil and stir until the sugar is dissolved. Boil for 1 minute. Remove from the heat and pour into the nut mixture. Add the vanilla and stir to combine. Allow to cool.

Using a 1 tablespoon cookie scoop, place four cookie balls on each baking sheet. If you do more than this, they will run together. Bake the cookies for 9–11 minutes or until golden brown and lacy. Remove the parchment paper or baking mat from the baking sheet and place on work surface to cool. Repeat the process until all cookies are baked and cooled.

In a bowl, whip the remaining ¼ cup of butter until light and airy. Add the confectioners' sugar and enough pineapple juice to a make frosting. Beat to combine. Add the chopped pineapple and coconut flakes.

Gently spoon frosting over one cookie. Sandwich together with a cookie of the same shape/size. Repeat the process with the remaining cookies. Place on a serving platter and serve.

GLUTEN-FREE VANILLEKIPFERL
(Almond Crescent Cookies)

Vanillekipferl is a traditional Christmas cookie originating in Austria, but it has become a popular holiday sweet in Germany, Czech Republic, Slovakia, and Hungary. As the story goes, way back in history, the Austro-Hungarian Empire repelled an invasion from the Ottoman Turks, partly thanks to bakers in Vienna who first raised the alarm. The bakers celebrated by creating these little cookies, shaped into crescents to symbolize the Turkish flag. I have made them gluten-free because I suffer from celiac disease. Even though these cookies are made with gluten-free flour, you would never be able to tell the difference.

CONTESTANT: SAMANTHA WILSON
HENDERSON, NV

2   cups gluten-free flour

1⅔   cup confectioners' sugar, divided use

¼   teaspoon salt

1½   cups ground raw almonds

1   egg yolk

1   tablespoon vanilla extract

1   cup unsalted butter, softened

Preheat the oven to 350°F. Line baking sheets with parchment paper or silicone baking mats.

In a large bowl, mix the flour, ⅔ cup of the confectioners' sugar, salt, and almonds. Mix these ingredients until evenly blended. Then add the egg yolk, vanilla, and butter. Knead all the ingredients together.

Once mixed and kneaded, start forming the dough into small balls (about a teaspoon in size). Mold each small dough ball into a crescent shape and carefully place the crescents on baking sheets.

Bake 8–11 minutes or until slightly brown. Allow to cool completely. Once cooled, liberally dust the crescent cookies with the remaining confectioners' sugar and serve.

SWEET & SAVORY ◆ **49**

PISTACHIO BLOSSOM
Cookies

My grandmother used to make an Armenian cookie called karabeech, *which was a buttery cookie stuffed with ground pistachios. The cookie itself wasn't very sweet, and as a result, it would be dipped in marshmallow fluff for some extra sweetness. My pistachio blossom cookies were inspired by my grandmother's recipe. The cookie incorporates all of the original flavors plus the added bonus of some delicious chocolate! Biting into this cookie and finding the hidden marshmallow cream is a delightful and tasty surprise!*

CONTESTANT: CAROLINE ZETJIAN
PORTER RANCH, CA

Cookie Dough

- 1 cup butter, softened
- 2 cups granulated sugar
- 2 teaspoons vanilla extract
- 3 cups all-purpose flour + additional for rolling

Sugar Syrup

- 1 tablespoon orange blossom water
- ½ cup sugar
- ¼ cup water

Marshmallow Cream

- 1 egg white
- ⅔ cup light corn syrup
- ¼ teaspoon salt
- ⅔ cup confectioners' sugar
- 2 teaspoons vanilla extract

Pistachio Topping

- 10 ounces pistachios, ground
- ¼ cup sugar
- 2 teaspoons orange blossom water

Chocolate Glaze

- ¼ cup heavy cream
- 4 ounces 60% cocoa/bittersweet chocolate

White Chocolate Coating

- 18 ounces white chocolate chips

Make the cookie dough. Cream the butter and sugar until fluffy. Stir in the vanilla. Add the flour and mix well. Form into a disk and refrigerate for about 30 minutes.

Make the sugar syrup. Mix together the orange blossom water, sugar, and water in a pot set over medium-high heat and bring to a boil. Once it boils, turn off the burner and allow the mixture to cool.

Preheat the oven to 350°F. Line baking sheets with parchment paper or silicone baking mats.

Remove the cookie dough from the refrigerator and roll the dough to about ¼ inch thick on a floured surface. Cut into shapes with cookie cutters. Place the cookies onto the baking sheets and cook for 15 minutes or until the edges are just lightly golden.

Remove the cookies from oven and allow to cool slightly. While they are still warm, brush the cookies lightly with the sugar syrup and allow to completely absorb and cool.

Make the marshmallow cream. Mix the egg white, corn syrup, and salt on high speed until fluffy and at the soft peak stage. Sift the confectioners' sugar into the mix and mix on low speed until thoroughly incorporated. Stir in the vanilla.

Make the pistachio topping. Toss the pistachios with the sugar and orange blossom water until evenly coated.

Make the chocolate glaze. Bring the heavy cream to a boil and remove from the heat. Stir in the chocolate until melted and fully incorporated. Allow to cool slightly.

Make the white chocolate coating. Melt the white chocolate chips in a double broiler or microwave. Using a decorating bag, pipe a thin layer of marshmallow cream onto the cookies. Dip the top of each cookie into the melted white chocolate and immediately sprinkle with the pistachio mix. Using a decorating bag, drizzle the top of each cookie with the chocolate glaze and allow to cool.

CHOCOLATE-COVERED ROCCOCO

This is a traditional holiday recipe that my grandmother used to make in Italy when I lived there as a child. It reminds me of the wonderful festivities and of the love, food, and family we celebrated. I don't have my grandma anymore, but I re-created her recipe, which I now share with my children and grandchildren. The best part is that these cookies are full of nutritious ingredients that make them a good-for-you snack!

CONTESTANT: ANTOINETTE SOLLA-CAPODICCI
SOUTHBURY, CT

Cookie Dough

- 2 cups whole almonds, toasted
- 1 cup dried fruit (figs, raisins, apricots)
- 4 cups all-purpose flour + addtional for rolling
- 1 cup granulated sugar
- ¼ cup honey
- ½ cup water
- 1 tablespoon allspice
- 2 teaspoons baking powder
- 1 teaspoon vanilla extract
- 1 teaspoon orange extract
- 1 teaspoon lemon extract
- Pinch of salt

Chocolate Glaze

- 1½ pounds bittersweet chocolate chips
- 1 tablespoon shortening

Preheat the oven to 350°F. Line baking sheets with parchment paper or silicone baking mats.

Make the cookie dough. Grind the toasted almonds in a food processor. Add the dried fruit and reduce to a paste. Blend the flour, sugar, honey, water, allspice, baking powder, vanilla, orange, and lemon extracts, and salt with a stand mixer or electric mixer on low speed until a well-mixed dough forms. The dough will be hard, but if it's too hard, add a little more water.

Turn the dough onto a lightly floured surface and separate into 12 equal pieces. Roll each piece into a rope and form a bagel-shaped cookie. Repeat with each piece. Place all the cookies on the baking sheets, evenly separated. Bake for 18 minutes. Cool on a wire rack.

Make the chocolate glaze. Melt the chocolate and shortening together in a microwave on 50 percent power or using a double boiler. Stir to combine.

Dip each cookie in the melted chocolate until evenly coated. Gently place on a wire rack and cool until the chocolate solidifies.

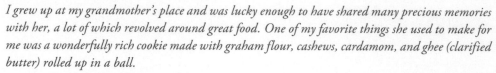

YUMMY TO THE CORE

I grew up at my grandmother's place and was lucky enough to have shared many precious memories with her, a lot of which revolved around great food. One of my favorite things she used to make for me was a wonderfully rich cookie made with graham flour, cashews, cardamom, and ghee (clarified butter) rolled up in a ball.

I've played around with Grandma's cardamom cookie recipe quite a bit, and I just happened to create Yummy to the Core, a vegan cookie recipe using vegan butter. It perfectly blends the taste of cardamom and almonds and adds a little surprising fruity twist in the core as the cookie melts in your mouth.

CONTESTANT: SANGAMITHRA NARASIMHAN
AUSTIN, TX

1 **cup all-purpose flour**
2 **tablespoons packed brown sugar**
1 **teaspoon ground cardamom**
½ **cup vegan butter**
½ **cup almonds, coarsely ground**
  Fruit jam (any flavor)
4 **tablespoons confectioners' sugar**

Add the flour, brown sugar, cardamom, and butter to a food processor. Pulse until a dough is formed. Add the coarsely ground almonds to the dough and knead it. The texture should feel chunky after the almonds are worked into the dough. Wrap dough with plastic wrap and freeze for 15 minutes.

Preheat the oven to 350°F. Line baking sheets with parchment paper or silicone baking mats. Form twelve 1½ inch balls of dough, and slice each ball into two halves. With your finger, press a light indentation into the middle of the sliced surface of half of each ball. Drop ¼ teaspoon of jam into each indentation. Seal the sliced ball of cookie dough with the other slice of the dough and smooth into a ball again. The idea is to have jam in the core of each cookie.

Bake the cookies for 13 minutes. When cool enough to handle but still warm, roll in confectioners' sugar. Serve!

TASTE OF TUSCANY

I came up with this recipe as the grand finale to an Italian dinner party I was throwing for a group of friends and family. I wanted to do something a little different, something that would incorporate the flavors of Tuscany and present beautifully. The red wine gives the cookies a gorgeous color and marries the sweetness of the brown sugar and figs with the savory rosemary and almond, highlighting the gooey balsamic figs.

CONTESTANT: JAMIE BROWN-MILLER
NAPA, CA

¾ cup balsamic vinegar

¾ cup packed brown sugar + additional for rolling

¾ cup dried figs, minced

⅔ cup olive oil

1 cup granulated sugar

1 large egg

2 tablespoons red wine

3 tablespoons finely minced rosemary, divided use

2¼ cups all-purpose flour

1 teaspoon baking powder

½ teaspoon baking soda

½ teaspoon salt

1 tablespoon almond extract

12 ounces mascarpone cheese

Preheat the oven to 375°F.

Stir the balsamic vinegar and brown sugar together in a small saucepan over high heat. Stir in the figs and bring to a boil. Reduce the heat to medium-high and boil the mixture until frothy. Reduce the mixture for 8 minutes, then pour into a heat-proof bowl to cool.

Line a large baking sheet with a sheet of parchment paper or a silicone baking mat and set aside.

Add the olive oil, granulated sugar, egg, and wine to a large bowl. Whisk to fully incorporate. Add half of the rosemary and stir to mix. Add the flour, baking powder, baking soda, and salt. Mix thoroughly.

Roll the dough into 1 inch balls, then roll the balls in a bowl of brown sugar. Place the balls onto the baking sheet about 4 inches apart, and flatten to ½ inch thick with your hand. Sprinkle with the remaining rosemary. Bake each batch for 8–10 minutes. Allow to cool. While the cookies and the fig mixture cool, stir the almond extract into the mascarpone cheese.

To assemble, spread the bottom side of half of the cookies with the mascarpone, about 1 tablespoon per cookie. Add 1 teaspoon of the fig mixture to the mascarpone on each cookie, then top with the remaining cookies, bottom sides to the fig mixture.

CHERRY HIDEAWAY
Cookies

When I first started baking cookies with my mom, every holiday season she always whipped out her favorite sugar cookie recipe. It was part of a little pamphlet that was older than the both of us combined. When she brought out the pamphlet, we would make the same cookie recipes it contained time and time again. But there was one in particular I always begged her to let me make, and every time she would say, "When you have kids, you can make that cookie for them." Years passed, and I did start having my own children. When I finally came looking for that little booklet, it had gone missing, so I had to come up with my own version that was equally delicious.

CONTESTANT: CATHERINE DAVIS
MARION, IL

⅔ cup vegetable shortening
¾ cup granulated sugar
1 egg
1 tablespoon milk
1 teaspoon vanilla extract
1¾ cups all-purpose flour
1 teaspoon baking powder
½ teaspoon salt
½ teaspoon baking soda
36 large maraschino cherries
8 ounces milk chocolate, chopped
½ cup shredded coconut

Preheat the oven to 350°F.

With an electric mixer or stand mixer, cream the shortening, sugar, egg, milk, and vanilla. Add the flour, baking powder, salt, and baking soda. Mix until combined. Drain the cherries on a paper towel and pat dry.

Wrap about 1 tablespoon of dough around each cherry and place an inch apart on a baking sheet. Bake for 10–13 minutes, until the edges just begin to brown.

Cool for 15 minutes. Melt the chocolate in a microwave-safe bowl. Dip half of each cookie in melted chocolate and sprinkle with coconut.

APRICOT WREATHS

A love for Christmas cookies, particularly German styles and flavors, influenced this cookie. I enjoy creating recipes and playing around with flavor profiles and concepts.

CONTESTANT: MAGGIE WARSZYCKI
LAGRANGEVILLE, NY

½ cup butter, softened
½ granulated sugar
2 eggs, divided use
1 teaspoon vanilla extract
2¼ cups all purpose flour
¼ cup almonds, finely ground
1 cup sliced almonds
½ cup apricot jam

Cream the butter and sugar until light and fluffy.

Add 1 egg and the vanilla. Slowly add the flour and ground almonds. Mix until combined. Wrap and refrigerate for at least 1 hour.

Preheat the oven to 350°F. Roll the dough to ¼ inch thickness and cut with a 2½ inch round cutter, adding a hole in one half of the shapes to create the tops of the cookies.

Beat the remaining egg and brush onto the cookie tops, then cover with sliced almonds. Bake for 10–15 minutes until golden. Once cooled, spread jam onto the cookie bottoms and gently press on the cookie tops, almond side up.

STRAWBERRY DREAM
Thumbprints

My grandmother made these cookies often when I was a little girl, but I never knew the recipe. Over the years my mother and I have experimented with different combinations of ingredients and finally came up with a perfect rendition of her delicious cookie! These are a favorite for all.

CONTESTANT: PATRICIA PORA
HARRISVILLE, RI

Cookie Dough
- 1 cup butter, softened
- ⅔ cup granulated sugar
- 1½ teaspoons strawberry extract
- 2 cups all-purpose flour
- 1 cup freeze-dried strawberries

Filling
- ½ cup butter, softened
- 1 cup confectioners' sugar
- 1 tablespoon strawberry syrup
- ¼ teaspoon strawberry extract

Topping
- ¼ cup white chocolate chips
- ⅛ teaspoon shortening

Make the cookie dough. Combine the butter with the sugar and strawberry extract in large bowl with an electric mixer or stand mixer on medium speed.

Add the flour slowly. Beat on low speed, being careful to scrape the sides of the bowl to ensure it is well mixed. Fold in the freeze-dried strawberries. Cover the dough and refrigerate for 45 minutes, or until the dough is firm enough to roll into balls.

Preheat the oven to 350°F.

Form the dough into 1-inch balls and place on an ungreased baking sheet. Using the end of a wooden spoon or your thumb, make indentations in the center of each ball. The edges may crack a little.

Bake 9–11 minutes or until the edges are light brown. Reshape the center of each cookie with the end of a wooden spoon. Place the cookies on a wire rack and cool completely, about 20 minutes.

Make the filling. Combine the butter, confectioners' sugar, strawberry syrup, and strawberry extract. Mix well. Spoon the filling into the center of each cookie.

Make the topping. Place the white chocolate chips and shortening in a microwave-safe bowl. Heat in the microwave on low power for 15-second intervals until melted. Stir well and transfer to a pastry bag. Drizzle the white chocolate over each cookie.

CINNAMON BANANA CHIP
Cookies

My mother gave me a version of this recipe many years ago. She's a great baker, and I've learned all about baking from her. I tried the recipe and added the mini chocolate chips. This brought the recipe up to a whole new level. These taste like a combo of banana muffins and a cookie, so they are great for breakfast too (wink, wink). I've been making these for many years now, and my best friend calls them Becky Cookies. Whenever I bring them over, her kids yell, "Are those Becky Cookies?" This has become my signature cookie, and after you taste them once, you'll be asking for more.

CONTESTANT: REBECCA BUFIS
KENDALL PARK, NJ

3 cups all-purpose flour
1 teaspoon baking soda
¼ teaspoon salt
1 cup softened butter
1¼ cups granulated sugar, divided use
¼ cup packed brown sugar
1 egg
1 large ripe banana
1 teaspoon ground cinnamon
6 ounces mini chocolate chips

Combine the flour, baking soda, and salt in a medium bowl; set aside. Beat together the butter, 1 cup of the sugar, and brown sugar in a large bowl until light and fluffy. Beat in the egg and banana until combined, then add to flour mixture and stir until combined. Stir in the chocolate chips. Cover and refrigerate 2 hours or overnight, until the dough is firm.

Preheat the oven to 350°F. Line baking sheets with parchment paper or silicone baking mats.

Combine the remaining ¼ cup sugar and cinnamon in a small bowl. Using a cookie scoop, shape the dough into 1 inch balls. Roll each ball in the cinnamon mixture. Place the balls 2 inches apart on baking sheets. Bake for 10–12 minutes or until lightly browned.

LEX'S LAVENDER
Shorties

I began making this recipe about six years ago. I love lavender anything and thought, Why not try it in my sugar cookie dough? *The worst it would do would be to make the house smell good! Well, they turned out amazing, tasting like shortbread with a unique twist, and are now my most requested cookie. They are even my four-year-old's favorite! They're simply delicious with a cup of hot tea or dipped in a glass of cold milk.*

CONTESTANT: ALEXIS BOYCE

SIOUX FALLS, SD

1 cup butter
1 cup granulated sugar
1 large egg
2 tablespoons pure almond extract
2¾ cups flour + additional for rolling
2 teaspoons baking powder
½ cup lavender buds + 2–3 tablespoons for topping

Preheat the oven to 350°F. Line baking sheets with parchment paper or silicone baking mats.

Cream the butter and sugar. Add the egg and almond extract and mix completely.

In a separate bowl, combine the flour, baking powder, and ½ cup of the lavender and mix slowly into butter mixture until thoroughly mixed. It will be a smooth, slightly sticky lump.

Dust your hands with extra flour and roll into 1 inch balls. Place the balls on baking sheets. Make a light indentation in the top of each ball with your thumb and sprinkle in a few lavender buds. Bake for 6–8 minutes, checking continually until the edges and bottoms are a light brown.

Let cool for 30 minutes.

LEMON BLUEBERRY
Delights

I have always tried to teach my children how wonderful it is to use local fruit and produce. This past year, I gave up sweets for Lent. About halfway through, I had a terrible sweet tooth, so I got the bright idea to start making cookie dough and freezing it. Baking is a favorite pastime of mine, so if I couldn't eat them, I would still prepare them. I looked in the freezer and found blueberries. This delicious recipe is now a family favorite.

CONTESTANT: SHARON SOTO
DWIGHT, IL

1   cup margarine

1   cup brown sugar

1   cup granulated sugar

½   cup Egg Beaters

2   teaspoons lemon extract

Zest and juice from 2 lemons, divided use

1½   cups + 2 tablespoons all-purpose flour, divided use

½   teaspoon baking powder

½   teaspoon salt

3   cups quick oats

1   cup blueberries (fresh or frozen)

1   cup confectioners' sugar

Cream together the margarine and both sugars with a stand mixer or electric mixer on medium speed until soft. Beat in the Egg Beaters, lemon extract, and half the zest.

In a separate bowl, combine 1½ cups of the flour, the baking powder, and the salt. Beat the flour mixture into the margarine mixture until combined. Add the oats. In a small bowl, toss the blueberries in the remaining 2 tablespoons of flour. Carefully fold the blueberries into the cookie dough.

Using a 1 ounce scoop, scoop cookie dough out onto a baking sheet. Refrigerate 1 hour. (The dough can also be frozen for later use.) Preheat the oven to 350°F. Line baking sheets with parchment paper or silicone baking mats. Bake for 15–18 minutes until the cookies are light in color.

While the cookies are baking, prepare the glaze. Mix the confectioners' sugar, the remaining lemon zest, and enough lemon juice to make a glaze of the desired consistency. Let the cookies cool 10 minutes, then drizzle with the lemon glaze.

NONNI'S ITALIAN WEDDING
Cookies

When my mother was a little girl and would attend family weddings, her best memory was of the Italian wedding cookies that would be passed out. Weddings were large family affairs, and adults and all their children would be included.

Over the years, Italian wedding cookies continued as an important tradition in our family. I learned that my own grandmother (my mother's mom) made the same wedding cookies for my parents' wedding. They also became the first cookie made during our Christmas holiday season. My brother is getting married in August, and I plan to bake these cookies for his wedding so we can continue the tradition.

CONTESTANT: ALEXIS BECKER
AKRON, OH

Cookie Dough

- 1 cup granulated sugar
- ¾ cup butter, softened
- 4 eggs
- 3 teaspoons vanilla extract
- 5 cups all-purpose flour
- 1 tablespoon baking powder
- ½ cup milk
- 1 teaspoon orange zest

Icing

- ½ cup butter, softened
- 3 cups confectioners' sugar
- 1 teaspoon vanilla extract
- ⅓ cup milk (approximate)
-    Sprinkles (optional)

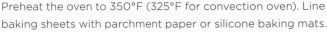

Preheat the oven to 350°F (325°F for convection oven). Line baking sheets with parchment paper or silicone baking mats.

Make the cookie dough. Cream together the sugar and butter until well blended. Mix in the eggs one at a time. Beat until light and fluffy, then add the vanilla. In a separate bowl, combine the flour and baking powder. Add the dry ingredients to the creamed mixture alternately with the milk. The dough will be the consistency of bread dough. Mix until well blended. Refrigerate for 10-15 minutes (do not refrigerate overnight).

Make the icing. While dough is chilling, mix the butter, confectioners' sugar, and vanilla. Add milk until the icing is the consistency you would use to frost a cake—it should be fluffy, not runny. Set aside.

Roll dough into round balls the size of approximately 1 heaping teaspoon (approximately 1 inch in diameter). Place each ball approximately 2-3 inches apart on a prepared baking sheet. Bake for approximately 10-12 minutes until lightly golden on the bottoms. The tops of the cookies should be firm. Remove from the oven and coat the top and sides of each cookie with icing while the cookies are warm. If desired, add colored sprinkles quickly before the icing cools.

CRANBERRY LIME SNOW
Cookies

Ever since I was a child, my mother and I have always loved to bake. She would always try to bake some fun themed cookies and sweets so that I would enjoy cooking with her. One day when we were thinking of some cookies that we could make for Christmastime, my mom decided that I could come up with my own recipe and she would come up with one. I wanted to make a recipe that was very festive with bright green and red colors for the season, so I decided that I would make a butter cookie that my mother used to make and add a Christmas flair to it. I also wanted to make the cookies look like snow, so the glaze on top added the frosty white look that I wanted.

CONTESTANT: ZACHARY WHITWORTH
ROEBUCK, SC

Cookie Dough

- 2 cups salted butter, softened
- 1⅓ cups granulated sugar
- 2 egg yolks
- 3 tablespoons lime zest
- 4 cups all-purpose flour
- 2 tablespoons lime juice

Icing

- 2 tablespoons whole milk
- 3 tablespoons lime juice
- 2 cups confectioners' sugar

Topping

- 1 cup finely chopped fresh cranberries
- Zest of 2–3 limes

Preheat the oven to 350°F. Line baking sheets with parchment paper or silicone baking sheets.

Make the cookie dough. Cream the butter and sugar. Add the egg yolks and mix well. Add the lime zest and flour and mix until just combined. Add the lime juice and mix until well combined.

Use a teaspoon or 1 inch cookie scoop to portion the dough, and roll each bit of dough into a ball. Place on baking sheets and bake for 12–14 minutes until very light brown. Let cool completely on wire racks before icing.

Make the icing. Whisk together the milk, lime juice, and confectioners' sugar. Add more milk or lime juice if necessary to reach a thick, pourable consistency.

Drizzle the icing on the cooled cookies and immediately top with chopped fresh cranberries and sprinkle with lime zest.

GLUTEN-FREE ROSE GARDEN
Shortbread Cookies

I grew up in the shadow of my mother, who was a professionally trained baker and gardener. She spent countless hours during the week and weekend maintaining her lavish flower garden. I remember smelling the fresh-cut flowers that my mom had placed in her favorite vase on our dining room table and thinking, Hmm, they smell so good, I could just eat them. Fast-forward many years and ta-da…an edible rose garden.

CONTESTANT: LUMA ABU-GHAZALEH
LA MESA, CA

Garnish

15–20 dried or fresh rose petals, depending on the petal size

2–3 tablespoons granulated sugar

Small pinch of ground cardamom

1 egg white

Cookie Dough

1 cup gluten-free flour + additional for rolling

⅓ cup very fine gluten-free brown rice flour

1 teaspoon xanthan gum

Pinch of salt

½ cup cold butter, cut into ½ × ½ inch cubes

1½–2 teaspoons rose water or orange blossom water

1 teaspoon freshly ground cardamom (about 6–8 cardamom pods)

2½ teaspoons dried rose petals, roughly chopped

½ cup confectioners' sugar

Make the garnish. Lay the rose petals flat on parchment or waxed paper. In a small bowl or cup, whisk the egg white until frothy. In a separate small bowl, mix the sugar and cardamom together. With a small and clean watercolor brush or pastry brush, paint both sides of the rose petals with the egg white wash. (If you don't have either brush, simply dip your finger in the egg white wash and use to paint both sides; do not dip the petal directly in the egg white wash.) Sprinkle both sides with the sugar mixture. Set the petals on a piece of parchment paper or waxed paper and let dry overnight.

Once dry, roughly chop the candied rose petals to use later for garnish.

Make the cookie dough. In a medium bowl, whisk the flours, xanthan gum, and salt together. Add the butter and rose or orange blossom water to the flour mixture and, with your fingers, work until it comes together and resembles chunky breadcrumbs (about 2 minutes).

In a separate bowl, whisk the cardamom, chopped rose petals, and confectioners' sugar together until evenly combined.

Add the confectioners' sugar mixture to the flour mixture. Combine with your hands until all ingredients start to come together and form a smooth dough. Avoid working it too much.

Flour a cool and clean surface and roll out dough until ½ inch think. Cut dough with your favorite cookie cutter shapes.

Line a baking sheet with parchment paper or a silicone baking mat and place the cut cookies 1 inch apart. Sprinkle the top of each cookie with the rose petal garnish and slightly tap the surface of each cookie to fuse the garnish and cookie together.

Refrigerate the trays for about 20–30 minutes until the cookies are cold and firm.

During that time, preheat the oven to 350°F.

Bake the cookies for about 20 minutes or until the edges are golden. Remove from the oven and let stand for about 5 minutes.

ITALIAN PIZZELLES

This is an old favorite recipe that has been in my family for many years. I remember my mother, Christina, making these cookies for Christmas, Easter, and weddings when I was a little girl. Although it is not a fancy cookie, it is delicious and calorie friendly. My family and friends agree that this is the best pizzelle cookie they have ever tasted.

CONTESTANT: ROSEMARIE SWIDERSKI
PITTSBURGH, PA

1 cup butter

1 cup granulated sugar

6 eggs

Zest of 1 orange

Zest of 2 lemons

1½ teaspoons anise oil

3 cups all-purpose flour

3 teaspoons baking powder

In a medium bowl, cream the sugar and butter. Mix in the eggs. Add the orange zest, lemon zest, and anise oil and mix well. Add the flour and baking powder. Mix well. Put 1 teaspoon of batter on both sides of pizzelle iron and cook about 20 seconds.

STAR
Cookies

My Greek nana would make these stars every holiday. The star shape is traditional. The cardamom addition is my adaptation, as we did not care for the brandy. Nana would watch them disappear faster than she could make them! As children it was difficult to wait for them to cool. It was even harder to sneak one into my mouth, as the telltale confectioners' sugar all over my face would get me caught every time!

CONTESTANT: LESLIE PONCE
MIAMI, FL

1½ cups butter, melted

2 egg yolks

¾ cup granulated sugar

1 cup finely chopped walnuts

¾ teaspoon salt

4 cups all-purpose flour + additional for rolling

1 teaspoon vanilla extract

¼ teaspoon ground cardamom

2 tablespoons brandy (optional)

Confectioners' sugar for dusting

Preheat the oven to 350°F.

Mix together the melted butter, egg yolks, and sugar. Add the walnuts, salt, flour, vanilla, cardamom, and brandy and mix by hand. Place the dough on a floured surface and press out to ½ inch thick.

Cut out shapes with a 2 inch star-shaped cookie cutter and place onto an ungreased baking sheet. Bake for 18 minutes Remove to a wire rack and let cool. When the cookies are cool, use a strainer to sprinkle confectioners' sugar over the tops of the cookies.

BOMB BREAKFAST COOKIES
(Blueberry Oatmeal Maple Bacon)

I'm the first to admit that being a cookie monster means that I often eat them for breakfast. When I was spending time with family in Montreal, where they share my love of everything maple, I came across maple sugar, which has the intoxicating smell and taste of rich, buttery breakfast, and I was inspired to use it with the savory combination of the breakfast champion: bacon.

CONTESTANT: JENNIFER NEWFIELD
LOS ANGELES, CA

8 ounces dried blueberries

1 cup hot water

5 tablespoons maple syrup, divided use

7 strips of smoked bacon

½ teaspoon + a pinch sea salt, divided use

3 cups old-fashioned oats, divided use

1½ cups all-purpose flour

1 teaspoon baking powder

½ teaspoon baking soda

1 cup butter, softened

¾ cup granulated maple sugar

¾ cup brown sugar

2 eggs

1 teaspoon vanilla extract

Combine the blueberries, hot water, and 1 teaspoon of the maple syrup. Set aside to plump.

Heat a skillet on medium heat and add the bacon. Cook 12–15 minutes until very crispy. Drain the fat into a bowl and reserve. Chop the bacon into small pieces, discarding any that are too fatty. Return the bacon pieces to the skillet, add 2 tablespoons of the maple syrup, and cook on medium-low heat until the syrup is thick and pieces are coated (about 3 minutes). Sprinkle in a pinch of sea salt, toss, and set the pieces aside to cool.

Pulse 1½ cups of the oats in a food processor until partially ground. Pour into a large bowl and add the remaining 1½ cups of oats, the flour, the baking powder, the baking soda, and ½ teaspoon of the salt. Whisk to combine and set aside.

With an electric mixer or stand mixer, mix the butter, 3 tablespoons of the reserved rendered bacon fat, the sugars, and cream until pale and blended. Add the eggs one at a time, then the vanilla and remaining 2 teaspoons of maple syrup.

Turn the mixer down to low speed and add the dry ingredients until almost combined. Drain the blueberries and add them to the mixture along with ½ of the maple bacon pieces. Stir in by hand.

Line a baking sheet with parchment paper or a silicone baking mat. Scoop the dough onto the baking sheet in 2 tablespoon portions close together. Flatten with the palm of your hand (the dough will be sticky) and divide the remaining bacon pieces on top of the cookies. Chill the dough until firm, either in the freezer for at least 30 minutes or in the refrigerator overnight.

When the dough is chilled, preheat the oven to 350°F. Bake cookies for 14–16 minutes, rotating the sheets halfway through, until edges are set.

CHERRY PECAN FUDGE
Cookies

For a Christmas gift I make cherry fudge for everyone in my husband's office. They loved it so much, I decided to make it into a cookie so that it can be enjoyed all year long.

CONTESTANT: ALIZA HEWITT
FAIRMONT, WV

- 2 tablespoons butter
- 12 ounces semisweet chocolate chips
- 4 ounces butterscotch chips
- ½ cup milk
- ⅔ cup granulated sugar
- 2 eggs
- 1 teaspoon vanilla extract
- 2 cups all-purpose flour
- 1 teaspoon baking powder
- ½ teaspoon salt
- 1 cup chopped pecans
- 1 cup dried cherries
- 2 cups boiling water
- Confectioners' sugar for dusting

Preheat the oven to 375°F. Line baking sheets with parchment paper or silicone baking mats.

In a double boiler, melt the butter, chocolate chips, butterscotch chips, and milk; set aside. With an electric mixer or stand mixer, beat the sugar, eggs, and vanilla until mixed.

In a separate bowl, whisk the flour, baking powder, and salt until combined. Add the dry ingredients to the wet ingredients, then add the chocolate mixture and pecans.

In a separate bowl, soak the cherries in the boiling water for 1 minute or until plump. Drain all the water from cherries and then add them to the cookie mixture. Refrigerate the dough for 15 minutes.

Use a small ice cream scoop to place dough on the prepared baking sheets, spacing them 2 inches apart. Bake for 8–10 minutes or until slightly firm. Cool and dust with powdered sugar.

Gluten-Free
ORANGE-FIG AMARETTI COOKIES

When I was diagnosed with celiac disease nearly eight years ago, I thought my cookie-eating days were over. But cookbook research led me to European-style cookies that were based on nuts and were naturally gluten-free and absolutely delicious. I created this recipe to use two fruits that we've always enjoyed around the holidays: figs and oranges.

CONTESTANT: SUZANNE BANFIELD
BASKING RIDGE, NJ

1 pound almond paste

1 cup granulated sugar, divided use

1 cup confectioners' sugar, divided use

2 tablespoons apricot jam

3 egg whites

½ cup finely chopped figs

1 tablespoon orange zest

Put the almond paste, ½ cup of the granulated sugar, and ½ cup of the confectioners' sugar in the bowl of a food processor. Pulse until it forms very fine crumbs. Add the apricot jam and egg whites, one at a time, and pulse to combine. Transfer to a medium bowl, and fold in the figs and orange zest. Refrigerate for at least 30 minutes.

Preheat the oven to 325°F. Line three baking sheets with parchment paper or silicone baking mats.

Spread the remaining ½ cup of the granulated sugar and ½ cup of the confectioners' sugar onto two plates. Use a 1-inch scoop or scant tablespoon to drop balls of dough into the granulated sugar. Roll each ball in the granulated sugar, then roll in confectioners' sugar. Use your hands to shape each into a smooth ball and place on baking sheet.

Bake for 25–28 minutes or until cookies are beautifully cracked on top and starting to get golden. Cool 10 minutes on the baking sheets, then remove to a wire rack to cool completely.

RUNNER-UP RECIPE

COFFEE BREAK

I was really into baking cupcakes and had been trying new flavors and combinations and fillings for a couple weeks. I wanted to work out one with a coffee theme, so that had been on my brain. One Saturday I woke up having dreamed of the idea for this cookie. I didn't remember all of the dream, but I remembered the flavors for the cookie. I made it right after breakfast, and after a few trusted tasters had a try and a few tweaks, this is what I ended up with. I still haven't made that cupcake!

RUNNER-UP: BECKY SCHENCK
CYPRESS, TX

- ¼ cup coffee-flavored liqueur
- ½ cup unsalted butter
- 2 tablespoons instant espresso powder
- 1½ cups chocolate chips
- 4 eggs
- ½ cup granulated sugar
- 1⅛ cups brown sugar
- ½ cup cocoa
- 2 cups all-purpose flour
- ½ teaspoon salt
- 1½ teaspoons baking powder
- 2¼ teaspoons vanilla extract
- 2 cups medium-fine chopped chocolate-covered espresso beans (a food processor works well for this)

Heat the coffee liqueur, butter, espresso powder, and chocolate chips in a double broiler until the chocolate is melted and the mixture is smooth. Set aside to cool slightly.

Preheat the oven to 375°F. Line baking sheets with parchment paper or silicone baking mats.

In a large bowl, beat the eggs, sugars, and cocoa. In a separate bowl, whisk together the flour, salt, and baking powder. Add to the egg mixture and mix completely. Add the melted chocolate mixture and mix well. Add the vanilla and chopped espresso beans.

This is a very soft dough. It is best to use a 2 tablespoon ice cream scoop to scoop balls onto the baking sheet. Bake for 10 minutes. Do not overbake; the cookies will be soft, chewy, and fudgy.

DOUBLE-CHOCOLATE CHERRY
Chews

As a child, I cherished the plates of holiday cookies that my family exchanged with the neighbors. It was a glimpse into the traditions of other households. My favorites, though, were the chocolate cherry cookies from my best friend's mom. The chewy cookies, topped with a maraschino cherry and a slick of fudgy chocolate frosting, were the ultimate holiday treat to my nine-year-old self. I've reimagined those flavors into this more sophisticated version that is crispy-edged with chewy interiors, dark with chocolate, and blinged out with boozy cherries.

CONTESTANT: JENNIFER BECKMAN
FALLS CHURCH, VA

¾ cup dried cherries, coarsely chopped

3 tablespoons amaretto liqueur, divided use

1 cup all-purpose flour

½ cup almond flour

½ cup unsweetened cocoa powder

½ teaspoon baking soda

½ teaspoon salt

¾ cup unsalted butter, room temperature

¾ cup packed brown sugar

½ cup granulated sugar

½ teaspoon almond extract

3 ounces bittersweet chocolate, coarsely chopped

Combine the dried cherries with 2 tablespoons of the amaretto and set aside to soak while you prepare the rest of the dough.

Whisk together the flour, almond flour, cocoa powder, baking soda, and salt in a bowl; set aside.

With an electric mixer or stand mixer, cream the butter with the sugars, beating 2–3 minutes until light and fluffy. Beat in the remaining tablespoon of amaretto and the almond extract. With the mixer on low speed, mix in the dry ingredients until well combined, then mix in the cherries and their liquid, and the chocolate.

Transfer the dough to a large sheet of parchment paper. Shape into a log about 16 inches long. Roll up the parchment to encase the dough and twist the ends. Refrigerate for at least 1 hour. The dough log can be further wrapped in plastic wrap and chilled for up to a week or frozen for up to two months.

Preheat the oven to 325°F. Line baking sheets with parchment paper or silicone baking mats. Unwrap the dough and slice into ½ inch rounds. Arrange on baking sheets and bake for 12 minutes until the tops of the cookies look dry, even though they will not yet be firm. Cool on trays for 5 minutes, then transfer to a wire rack until fully cooled. Store in an airtight container at room temperature.

MINI DOUBLE-CHOCOLATE MINT
Cookies

When I was growing up, a meal wasn't complete without something sweet at the end. My mom kept peppermint patties or chocolate mints in her purse for restaurant dinners, but if we were at home, cookies were the dessert favorite. I've continued this tradition as an adult and bake a batch of cookies at least once a week. I have a weakness for chocolate, and during the holidays I add a little splash of peppermint to my hot chocolate for a seasonal touch. While making a batch of cookies this Christmas, I added some peppermint extract on a whim to my cookie batter, and these delicious treats were born.

CONTESTANT: DANIELLE GOLDIE
CAMARILLO, CA

2   cups all-purpose flour
¼   cup unsweetened cocoa powder
1   teaspoon baking soda
1   teaspoon kosher salt
1   cup unsalted butter, room temperature
¾   cup granulated sugar
¾   cup light brown sugar
2   large eggs, room temperature
1   teaspoon vanilla extract
1   teaspoon peppermint extract
12 ounces semisweet mini chocolate chips

Preheat the oven to 375°F. Line two baking sheets with parchment paper or silicone baking mats.

In a medium bowl, combine the flour, cocoa powder, baking soda, and salt. Set aside.

With an electric mixer or stand mixer, beat the butter and sugars until light and fluffy (approximately 3 minutes). Add the eggs one at a time, and beat well after each addition. Add the vanilla and peppermint extracts and beat until combined. With the mixer on low speed, gradually add the flour mixture, mixing until just combined. Add the chocolate chips and mix on low speed until evenly distributed.

Drop rounded teaspoons of cookie dough 1 inch apart on baking sheets. Bake approximately 6–8 minutes until cookies are set and slightly crisp around the edges.

Allow the cookies to cool on the baking sheet for 2–4 minutes and then transfer them to wire racks.

Enjoy!

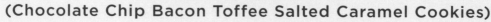

HOPPERDOODLES
(Chocolate Chip Bacon Toffee Salted Caramel Cookies)

Last July I was on a cookie-making binge and was seeking new and creative inspiration. I posted a cookie contest on Facebook, asking my friends to submit their favorite cookie flavor ideas. I chose my top five favorite ideas, and then made a survey for everyone to vote for their favorite of the five. My cousin Peter submitted the idea for Chocolate Chip Bacon Toffee Salted Caramel Cookies, and the masses (myself included) couldn't resist! Peter actually goes by the nickname Hopper, and thus the Hopperdoodle was born.

CONTESTANT: SARAH COHAN
BOSTON, MA

8 medium slices of bacon (not thick cut; approximately ½ pound)

11 tablespoons unsalted butter, divided use

¾ cup packed dark brown sugar

½ cup granulated sugar

2 teaspoons vanilla extract

1 large egg, room temperature

1 large egg yolk, room temperature

2 cups all-purpose flour

½ teaspoon baking soda

1 teaspoon salt

½ cup toffee bits

½ cup mini chocolate chips

16 caramels, cut into eighths

1 tablespoon sea salt

Preheat the oven to 375°F. Line a rimmed baking sheet with aluminum foil, then lay the bacon flat, ensuring that the strips do not touch. Bake until browned and crispy, 15-20 minutes, depending on your oven.

Drain the bacon on paper towels. Reserve 3 tablespoons of the bacon grease and refrigerate to cool slightly (it's all right if it solidifies a bit); discard the rest. Once the bacon is cool, crumble or chop it into tiny pieces and set it aside in a bowl.

In a small saucepan, brown 7 tablespoons of the unsalted butter by melting it over medium heat until it gets foamy on top. After the foam subsides, start swirling the pan every 15 seconds and cook until it stops popping loudly and you see brown bits accumulating on the bottom of the pan. Cook it 30 seconds longer—make sure you get those bits good and brown, or even black! Add the remaining 4 tablespoons of butter and the reserved 3 tablespoons of bacon grease, stirring gently to combine. Pour into a bowl, making sure to scrape out all the little dark bits with a spatula.

Add the brown sugar, granulated sugar, and vanilla. Using the whisk attachment of a stand mixer or electric mixer, mix on high speed until combined (60–90 seconds). Add the egg and egg yolk; whisk on high speed 30 seconds and let stand 3 minutes. Repeat that whisking/standing process twice more: whisk 30 seconds, let stand 3 minutes, whisk 30 seconds, and let stand 3 minutes.

While you're waiting, whisk together the flour, baking soda, and salt in a separate bowl by hand.

Whisk the sugar/egg mixture on high speed 30 seconds again, then switch to a paddle attachment to slowly mix in the dry ingredients on low speed (or fold in by hand with a spatula). Mix until just barely combined, then scrape down the sides of the bowl with a spatula.

Add the toffee bits, chocolate chips, caramel pieces, and the bacon bits. Mix on low speed for 10–15 seconds, or fold in with a spatula. If using a stand mixer, avoid overmixing.

Using an ice cream scoop, or a ¼ cup measure, scoop the dough into balls onto a baking sheet lined with waxed paper. Sprinkle each cookie with a pinch of sea salt, evenly distributing it as much as possible. You may not use the entire 1 tablespoon of salt for the batch. If the salt is rolling off the cookies, press it on gently with your fingertips.

Refrigerate for at least 2 hours or overnight, or freeze for 1 hour. You can also freeze them for 30 minutes and then put them in a gallon freezer zip-seal bag to freeze for baking at a later date. The dough will be good approximately 6 months in the freezer, and you can bake the cookies without thawing by adding approximately 2–4 minutes to the bake time.

When ready to bake, preheat the oven to 350°F. Line baking sheets with parchment paper or silicone baking mats and place the cookies at least 3 inches apart. Bake no more than eight at a time on an oversized baking sheet (20 × 16 inches). Place the sheet in the middle of your oven and bake only one sheet at a time. Keep the rest of the dough chilled until the next tray is ready to go in. Start checking the cookies at 10 minutes (though they may take 12–14 minutes in total)—they are done when the edges start to brown or crack and the center just barely doesn't look raw anymore. Don't overbake! They'll continue cooking a bit as they cool on the baking sheet. Cool on the baking sheet for 10 minutes, then transfer to a wire rack to cool completely.

DOUBLE DELIGHT CHOCOLATE
Thumbprints

A few years ago, my granddaughters started to help me bake my cookies for Christmas. This year, I put them in charge of coming up with a new cookie to make. One day when they were on the Barnes & Noble website, they spotted the flyer for the contest and said that I should enter. When they came over to my house to bake our Christmas cookies, we came up with the perfect recipe for our new cookie. A chocolate thumbprint cookie with peppermint cream cheese frosting. I came up with the name Double Delight because my granddaughters are identical twins, and the cookie we created has two delicious flavors combined together to form a delight in your mouth.

CONTESTANT: FAYE KREIDER
LEBANON, PA

Cookie Dough

- ⅔ cup butter
- ½ cup granulated sugar
- ¼ cup unsweetened cocoa powder
- ¼ teaspoon baking soda
- ⅛ teaspoon salt
- 1 egg
- 1 teaspoon vanilla extract
- 1¼ cups all-purpose flour
- ¾ cup holiday baking sprinkles (make sure they are baking sprinkles so that they won't melt in the oven)

Icing

- 1 cup confectioners' sugar, sifted
- 8 ounces cream cheese, softened
- 4 tablespoons butter, softened
- ½ teaspoon peppermint extract
- Mint chocolates for topping

Make the cookie dough. Beat the butter with an electric mixer or stand mixer on medium to high speed for 30 seconds. Add the sugar, cocoa powder, baking soda, and salt and beat until combined. Beat in the egg and vanilla until combined. Beat in as much of the flour as you can with the mixer. Stir in the remaining flour with a wooden spoon. Cover and refrigerate the dough for 1 hour or until it is easy to handle.

Preheat the oven to 350°F. Line baking sheets with parchment paper or silicone baking mats.

Once the dough is chilled, shape it into 1 inch balls. Roll each ball in sprinkles. Place balls 2 inches apart on prepared baking sheets. Press your thumb into the center of each ball. Bake for 7–9 minutes or until the edges are firm.

Make the icing. While the cookies are baking, mix the confectioners' sugar, cream cheese, butter, and peppermint extract with an electric mixer or stand mixer until creamy.

When the cookies are done, remove them from oven and make sure that all of your thumbprints are still there. (If not, make them bigger with the back of a spoon.) Let them cool for about 30 minutes. Once the cookies are cool, place a mint chocolate in each thumbprint and pipe the icing into the center and on top of the chocolate.

HOT CHOCOLATE
Cookies

Hot chocolate is one of my favorite drinks, and it's even better in cookie form. I came up with the idea when I was stuck outside in the cold waiting for a delayed train on a winter night.

CONTESTANT: KELLY THOMAS

FOLCROFT, PA

1¾ cups all-purpose flour

⅓ cup hot chocolate mix

½ teaspoon salt

½ teaspoon baking soda

¼ cup unsalted butter

½ cup granulated sugar

⅓ cup packed brown sugar

1 egg

2 tablespoons 2% milk

½ teaspoon vanilla extract

1 cup mini marshmallows

Preheat the oven to 350°F. Line baking sheets with parchment paper or silicone baking mats.

In a medium bowl, stir together the flour, hot chocolate mix, salt, and baking soda. Set aside.

In a large bowl, cream together the butter and both sugars until light and fluffy. Add in the egg, milk, and vanilla and mix until fully incorporated. Slowly add the flour mixture to the sugar mixture. Mix until well blended.

Roll the dough into balls roughly the size of a tablespoon and place on baking sheets. Bake for 10 minutes or until slightly firm. As soon as you remove the cookies from the oven, place marshmallows on top of the cookies and press down lightly. The marshmallows will start to melt into the tops of the cookies.

After cooling for a few minutes on baking sheets, transfer the cookies to a wire rack to cool completely.

RED WINE, ROSEMARY, AND DARK CHOCOLATE
Cookies

I enjoy developing recipes for baked goods, most especially cookies that are unique but still have a familiar and inviting taste. These Red Wine, Rosemary, and Dark Chocolate Cookies are my grown-up version of the beloved classic chocolate chip cookie we know so well. These cookies were conceived to satisfy the sophisticated but comforting taste I had been craving.

CONTESTANT: KRIS GALICIA BROWN
SAN DIEGO, CA

2　cups all-purpose flour
¾　cup ground walnuts
1　teaspoon baking powder
1　teaspoon baking soda
½　cup unsalted butter, room temperature
½　cup granulated sugar
½　cup packed brown sugar
1　egg
1　teaspoon vanilla extract
1　tablespoon finely chopped fresh rosemary
¼　cup red wine
1　cup dark chocolate chips

In a medium bowl, whisk together the flour, walnuts, baking powder, and baking soda.

With an electric mixer or stand mixer, cream the butter and both sugars. Add the egg, vanilla, and rosemary, then beat until completely combined.

Add the dry ingredients to the wet mixture one cup at a time until combined, scraping the sides of the bowl as needed. Add the red wine and combine at a low speed until it's swirled in. Stir in the dark chocolate chips until evenly distributed.

Using a spatula, gather the dough into the middle of the bowl. Cover the ball of dough with plastic wrap and refrigerate for at least 3 hours.

Preheat the oven to 350°F. Line a baking sheet with parchment paper or a silicone mat. Using a cookie scoop, portion out the cookie dough and place each portion on the baking sheet about 2 inches apart. Prepare only 1 dozen at a time, and keep the remaining dough refrigerated until ready to bake.

Bake for 10–12 minutes on the oven's middle rack. The edges should be just slightly golden. Let cool on the baking sheet for a couple of minutes and transfer to wire racks to cool completely.

CHOCOLATE ESPRESSO
Flats

My parents would go nuts every year making cookies for the holidays, and this recipe is one that was made every year. We've been tweaking it since I was a kid: My mom changed it up, and then when I started doing the baking I added my own little tweaks, like the vanilla, coffee, and cinnamon. My tweaks helped to bring out the coffee flavor more and make it more than a typical chocolate cookie.

CONTESTANT: ANGELA RIZZA
MAHOPAC, NY

4 ounces semisweet baking chocolate

1 cup butter, softened

½ cup granulated sugar

½ cup dark brown sugar

1 egg

¼ teaspoon salt

1 teaspoon ground cinnamon

1 teaspoon vanilla extract

3 tablespoons strong brewed coffee

2 tablespoons instant espresso powder, ground superfine with a mortar

2 cups all-purpose flour

Baker's brand dipping chocolate

Melt the baking chocolate in a microwave-safe cup, stirring every 15 seconds to avoid burning.

With an electric mixer or stand mixer, cream the butter with the sugars until fluffy. Add the egg, salt, cinnamon, vanilla, coffee, and espresso powder and combine. Add the flour gradually and mix. Cover and refrigerate for about an hour or until easy to handle.

Shape the dough into two rolls, each about 6 inches long. Wrap and refrigerate for at least 6 hours or overnight.

Preheat the oven to 350°F. Line baking sheets with parchment paper or silicone baking mats. Slice the rolls into ¼ inch slices, place on baking sheets, and bake for 10–12 minutes. Place on a wire rack to cool. Once cooled, dip each cookie halfway in the dipping chocolate and let it set on waxed paper.

BEST EVER DARK CHOCOLATE CHIP
Cookies

I grew up with a family that loved chocolate, especially chocolate chip cookies. This cookie recipe came about after testing dozens of different combinations to master my own chocolate chip cookie. Anytime I stray from this recipe, my testers still prefer this recipe over anything else, so I know that it has been tested solidly and cannot be beaten.

CONTESTANT: RACHEL SEEDORF
PATCHOGUE, NY

1 teaspoon salt

1 teaspoon baking powder

2½ cups all-purpose flour

1 cup salted butter, room temperature

¾ cup light brown sugar

¾ cup granulated sugar

1 egg

1 egg yolk

2 tablespoons maple syrup

2 teaspoons vanilla extract

1 cup dark chocolate, chopped (you can also use dark chocolate chunks or morsels)

Sift the salt, baking powder, and flour together in a medium bowl. Set aside.

With an electric mixer or stand mixer, mix together the butter and the sugars on medium speed until creamed together. Add in the egg and egg yolk and mix until just combined. Add in the maple syrup and vanilla and mix well.

With the mixer on low speed, gradually add the flour mixture in ½ cup increments until all is mixed in well.

Add the dark chocolate and then refrigerate the dough for a minimum of 4 hours (up to 24 hours).

Preheat the oven to 350°F. Line baking sheets with parchment paper or silicone baking mats.

Using a cookie scoop, form the dough into balls slightly larger than what the scoop provides (about 1½ inches around) and place on the baking sheets. Keep the dough balls high and round; do not flatten them.

Place the baking sheet on the middle rack in the oven and bake for 8–10 minutes, or until the edges begin to turn slightly golden. Bake only one sheet at a time.

Remove the baking sheet and allow the cookies to cool for 2 minutes. Carefully transfer the cookies from the baking sheet to a wire rack. Repeat the process until all of the dough has been used.

Gluten-Free
SALTED CHOCOLATE DREAM COOKIES

Several years back, a doctor misdiagnosed me with celiac disease. I went gluten-free that very day. For many years, I didn't eat sweets because there just weren't any good-tasting gluten-free products on the market. I was then on the baking path to a good gluten-free cookie. Even though I no longer have to eat gluten-free, I still make this recipe. The greatest thing is, no one knows that they are gluten-free. For a different twist on these cookies, simply cover one caramel or square with the dough, flatten a bit, and bake just like the instructions read.

CONTESTANT: CHERA LITTLE
CEDAR PARK, TX

1	cup pecan pieces
1	cup sliced almonds
3	cups confectioners' sugar
1	cup granulated sugar
1½	cups unsweetened cocoa powder
3½	teaspoons Himalayan pink sea salt
1	teaspoon instant coffee granules
1	teaspoon ground cinnamon
½	teaspoon smoked paprika
4	ounces bittersweet chocolate, chopped
8	egg whites

Preheat the oven to 325°F. Line baking sheets with parchment paper or silicone baking mats.

Toast the pecans and almonds in a large nonstick skillet over medium-high heat until slightly brown. Remove and let cool. In a large bowl, combine the sugars, cocoa powder, salt, coffee granules, cinnamon, and paprika. Stir in the chocolate and the nuts. Add the egg whites and mix until just combined.

Drop the dough by the heaping tablespoon onto baking sheets. Bake for 20–25 minutes or until the tops begin to form small cracks.

The Best of Both Worlds:
CHOCOLATE CHIP AND PECAN COOKIES

I am a stay-at-home supermom of 2½-year-old twins and a six-month-old baby. I am now on a mission to create the best chocolate chip cookie you can find in Brooklyn. I want to be the "sugar mama" of cookies! I was inspired by my favorite Food Network, Cooking Channel, and YouTube chefs to make these cookies, and I tested and combined various ingredients until I landed on this combination.

CONTESTANT: MILLIE MASSA
BROOKLYN, NY

1   cup butter, softened
½   cup packed brown sugar
½   cup granulated sugar
1   large egg, beaten
1   teaspoon pure vanilla extract
1¾ cups all-purpose flour
12 ounces semisweet chocolate chips
½   cup raw pecan pieces
    Coarse sea salt for sprinkling
    (optional)

Preheat the oven to 350°F. Line two baking sheets with parchment paper or silicone baking mats.

With an electric mixer or stand mixer, cream the butter and sugars until smooth and well combined, about 3 minutes. Slowly add the egg and continue to mix for 3 minutes until well combined. Add the vanilla and mix for 2 more minutes. Add the flour and combine to form a dough. Once the dough is well combined, add the chocolate chips and pecans and mix until evenly distributed throughout the dough, about 2 minutes.

Scoop tablespoon-size portions of the dough into your hands, roll into balls, and place onto the prepared baking sheets about 2 inches apart. Bake until golden but still soft in the center, about 10–12 minutes, depending on how chewy or crunchy you like your cookies or baking mats. Transfer the hot cookies, still on parchment paper or baking mats, to a wire rack to cool. Sprinkle sea salt on each cookie if desired.

MAMAW'S CHOCOLATE CARAMEL DELIGHT
Cookies

My mamaw used to make these cookies. As a child, I wondered how Mamaw got that caramel in the middle of the cookie without it melting out in the oven. As I got older, I realized that the dough served as a protector and allowed it to melt just enough. When I make these, they never last more than a day around our house. It would be an honor to share these wonderful cookies with the world and thank my 88-year-old mamaw, who still lives by herself and bakes each week!

CONTESTANT: STACEY RHODES
CONROE, TX

2¼ cups all-purpose flour

¾ cup unsweetened cocoa powder

1 teaspoon baking soda

1 cup + 1 tablespoon granulated sugar, divided use

1 cup firmly packed brown sugar

1 cup butter, softened

2 teaspoons vanilla extract

2 eggs

1 cup chopped pecans, divided use

48 chewy caramel candies in milk chocolate, unwrapped

4 ounces vanilla-flavored candy coating (optional)

Preheat the oven to 375°F.

In a small bowl, combine the flour, cocoa powder, and baking soda. Blend well and set aside. In a large bowl, beat 1 cup of the sugar, the brown sugar, and the butter until light and fluffy. Add the vanilla and eggs and beat well. Add the flour mixture and blend well. Stir in ½ cup of the pecans. In a small bowl, combine the remaining ½ cup pecans and 1 tablespoon sugar.

For each cookie, with floured hands, shape about 1 tablespoonful dough around 1 caramel candy, covering the candy completely. Press one side of each ball into the pecan mixture. Place the dough, nut side up, 2 inches apart on baking sheets.

Bake for 8–10 minutes or until set and slightly cracked. Cool 2 minutes, then remove from the baking sheets and cool completely on a wire rack. If desired, melt the candy coating in a small saucepan over low heat, stirring constantly until smooth. Drizzle over the cooled cookies.

CHOCO-POCALYPSE MINT
Cookies

Have you ever wondered how much chocolate you could pack into a cookie and still have it hold together? After a whole lot of experimenting, I found the answer. Using three different types of chocolate plus chocolate mints, these Choco-Pocalypse Mint Cookies were born. With an apocalypse of chocolate (and only ½ cup of flour), this isn't your momma's chocolate cookie.

CONTESTANT: LINDSAY WEISS
OVERLAND PARK, KS

½ cup unsalted butter, cut into pieces

9 ounces best-quality bittersweet chocolate, finely chopped

3 ounces best-quality unsweetened chocolate, finely chopped

½ cup all-purpose flour

½ teaspoon baking powder

¼ teaspoon salt

3 large eggs, room temperature

1¼ cups superfine granulated sugar*

2 teaspoons pure vanilla extract

2 cups semisweet chocolate chips

1 cup coarsely chopped chocolate mint candies

*If you don't have superfine sugar at home, just put regular sugar in your blender or food processor and process for 15 seconds or so.

Preheat the oven to 350°F. Line baking sheets with parchment paper or silicone baking mats.

Melt the butter in a double boiler. Once the butter is melted, add the bittersweet and unsweetened chocolate and stir until melted and smooth. Remove the bowl from the heat and let cool slightly. Combine the flour, baking powder, and salt in a medium bowl and set aside.

With an electric mixer or stand mixer, beat the eggs until foamy, about 30 seconds. Increase the speed to high and gradually add the sugar, then the vanilla. Continue beating until the eggs are very thick and pale yellow, about 3 minutes. Reduce the mixer speed to medium and beat in the cooled chocolate, making sure it is completely incorporated. Reduce the mixer speed to low and gradually add the flour mixture.

Stir in the chocolate chips and chopped chocolate mint candies by hand. Let the dough stand for 5 minutes. The dough will be rather wet.

Using a 1½ tablespoon cookie scoop, scoop the dough onto the baking sheets, placing the cookies about 2 inches apart. Bake until the cookies are just set (centers should appear underdone but will firm up upon cooling), 11–14 minutes. Let cool right on the baking sheets.

TRIPLE CHOCOLATE MOCHA
Macs

I love to bake and have been creating recipes for many years. It gives me great joy to use my coworkers as guinea pigs! I've always thought chocolate and coffee are such a good combination and came up with this recipe to incorporate the two flavors. I think the crunchy saltiness of the macadamia nuts goes well with the chocolaty coffee flavor.

CONTESTANT: CINDY JACOBSON
PORTLAND, OR

1½ cups all-purpose flour

6 tablespoons unsweetened cocoa powder

1 teaspoon baking powder

½ teaspoon salt

¾ cup unsalted butter, softened

¾ cup packed light brown sugar

½ cup granulated sugar

2 eggs

1 teaspoon coffee extract

1 cup semisweet chocolate chips

3 ounces dark chocolate espresso bean candy bar, chopped in small pieces

½ cup dry-roasted macadamia nuts

Preheat the oven to 350°F.

In a medium bowl, mix together the flour, cocoa powder, baking powder, and salt. Set aside.

In a large bowl, beat the butter and both sugars together. Add the eggs, one at a time, beating until incorporated. Add the coffee extract and mix. Add the flour mixture a little at a time to the butter mixture. Mix until well incorporated, scraping down the sides of the bowl as needed. Fold in the chocolate chips, chopped candy bar, and macadamia nuts.

Drop by the tablespoon onto an ungreased baking sheet. Bake for 9–10 minutes. Don't overbake. Let cool for 2–3 minutes before removing to a wire rack to cool completely. Store in an airtight container.

SALTED ALMOND TRIPLE-CHOCOLATE
Rocky Road Cookies

These cookies were inspired by a family trip to the Smoky Mountains several years ago. My husband would joke around with the kids, telling them bears were especially fond of marshmallows. When we were making cookies, my youngest daughter suggested we add mini marshmallows to possibly encourage a bear sighting. To our surprise, later in the night there was a black bear outside our window!

CONTESTANT: NAYLET LAROCHELLE
MIAMI, FL

2 cups semisweet chocolate chips

¼ cup + ⅓ cup cream, divided use

⅛ cup + 1 tablespoon butter, divided use

1½ cups light brown sugar

3 eggs

1 teaspoon vanilla extract

1½ cups all-purpose flour

⅓ cup unsweetened cocoa powder

1 teaspoon baking powder

¼ teaspoon salt

1½ cups milk chocolate chips

1 cup chopped roasted and salted almonds

3–4 cups mini marshmallows, as needed

1½ cups dark chocolate chips

Fleur de sel or kosher salt, for sprinkling

Preheat the oven to 350°F. Line a large rimmed baking sheet with parchment paper or silicone baking mats.

In a medium saucepan over medium-low heat, combine the semisweet chocolate chips and ¼ cup of the cream. Cook, stirring occasionally, until the chocolate is melted and smooth. Remove from the heat and let cool slightly.

In a large bowl, beat ½ cup of the butter until light and fluffy. Beat in the brown sugar. Add the eggs, one at a time, beating in between each addition. Add the vanilla and about one-third of the slightly cooled melted chocolate and beat until just combined. Add the remaining melted chocolate and beat until just combined.

In a large bowl, combine the flour, cocoa powder, baking powder, and salt. Add the flour mixture to the chocolate mixture and beat until combined. Stir in the milk chocolate chips.

Drop the dough by rounded teaspoons about 2 inches apart on prepared baking sheet. Bake 6 minutes. Remove from the oven. Top each cookie with about 1 rounded teaspoon of almonds and 4–5 marshmallows. Return to the oven and bake an additional 2–3 minutes. Cool on the baking sheet 3 minutes, then transfer to a wire rack to cool completely.

In a medium saucepan over low heat, combine the dark chocolate chips, remaining ⅓ cup cream, and remaining 1 tablespoon butter. Stir until smooth and melted. Drizzle onto the cookies and sprinkle with a pinch of fleur de sel or kosher salt. Let the chocolate set before serving.

Let It Snow White Chocolate
VANILLA CAPPUCCINO COOKIES

My favorite gift of all time was a Christmas gift I received from my husband: a shiny black KitchenAid mixer. If I could bake one thing for the rest of my life, it would be cookies. So, I spend my days tweaking and creating new cookie flavors. This one was inspired by a bakery in California, and I knew I had to create it myself. It is full of classic holiday flavors: warm vanilla cappuccino by the fire, roasted marshmallows, and rich caramel all wrapped in a buttery cookie.

CONTESTANT: MELISSA STADLER
GILBERT, AZ

1 cup + 1 tablespoon butter, cut into cubes, divided use

¾ cup brown sugar

¾ cup granulated sugar

2 eggs

2 teaspoons bourbon vanilla bean paste or pure vanilla extract

3 tablespoons vanilla cappuccino powder

1 tablespoon nonfat powdered milk

2¾ cups all-purpose flour

½ teaspoon baking soda

½ teaspoon baking powder

1 teaspoon salt

1½ cups white chocolate chunks, divided use

1½ cups mini marshmallows

1 cup caramel bits

1 tablespoon butter

Preheat the oven to 400°F. Line baking sheets with parchment paper or silicone baking mats.

In a large bowl, cream 1 cup of the butter and the sugars for 4 minutes until light and fluffy. Add the eggs one at a time, mixing after each one. Add the vanilla bean paste or extract and stir until incorporated. Stir in the vanilla cappuccino powder, powdered milk, flour, baking soda, baking powder, and salt. Stir in 1 cup of the white chocolate chunks, the mini marshmallows, and the caramel bits.

Drop the dough by rounded tablespoons onto baking sheets. Bake for 8–10 minutes or until lightly golden brown on the edges. Meanwhile, in heat-resistant bowl, add the remaining ½ cup white chocolate chunks and 1 tablespoon butter. Heat over a double boiler or in the microwave on low power for 15-second increments. Drizzle the cookies with the melted white chocolate.

TREAT FOR SANTA
Cookies

Every year I try to come up with a different recipe than the traditional cookie or dessert. This year I was hosting a dinner party and wanted to have an interactive dessert, so I came up with this one. Kids and adults alike loved this cookie. The sipping, and dipping, and was fun and delicious for all!

CONTESTANT: ISABEL MINUNNI
POUGHKEEPSIE, NY

Cookie Dough

- 8 ounces dark chocolate chips
- 1 cup all-purpose flour
- ½ cup dark cocoa powder
- 2 teaspoons baking powder
- ¼ teaspoon salt
- 1 teaspoon instant coffee
- ½ cup unsalted butter, room temperature
- 1½ cups granulated sugar
- 2 large eggs
- 1 teaspoon vanilla extract
- ⅓ cup milk
- 1 cup confectioners' sugar

Filling

- 1½ cups butter
- 3 cups confectioners' sugar
- 1⅓ cups marshmallow topping
- Pinch salt
- 1 teaspoon vanilla extract
- ⅓ cup milk
- ½ cup crushed hazelnuts
- 2 cups chopped hazelnuts
- Caramel sauce for drizzle
- Sea salt for topping

Preheat the oven to 350°F. Line baking sheets with parchment paper or silicone baking mats.

Make the cookie dough. Melt the chocolate chips over a double boiler. Set aside to cool. In a medium bowl, sift together the flour, cocoa powder, baking powder, salt, and instant coffee.

With an electric mixer or stand mixer fitted with the paddle attachment, beat the butter and sugar on medium-high speed until light and fluffy. Add the eggs, one at a time, combining well. Add the vanilla and melted chocolate. With the mixer on low speed, alternate adding the dry ingredients and milk to the wet ingredients, starting and ending with dry ingredients, until just combined. Divide the dough in half and form each half into a log. Wrap each log with plastic wrap. Refrigerate until chilled (about 1 hour).

Cut the logs into pieces, forming 1 inch round balls, then coat each ball with confectioners' sugar. Place the cookies on the baking sheet and bake until cookies have flattened and the sugar splits, 12 minutes. Remove from the oven and transfer onto a wire rack to cool completely.

Make the filling. With an electric mixer or stand mixer, combine the butter, confectioners' sugar, marshmallow topping, salt, and vanilla and mix on medium speed until combined. Add the milk as needed slowly, with the mixer on low speed, until you achieve a thick, creamy consistency.

In a separate bowl, combine the crushed and chopped hazelnuts. Evenly spread filling on half of the cooled cookies and top with the remaining cookies to make sandwich cookies. Roll the cookie edges in the mixed nuts to coat the filling. Drizzle each cookie with caramel and sprinkle with salt.

TRIPLE-CHOCOLATE RED VELVET PEPPERMINT
Crinkle Cookies

These Triple-Chocolate Red Velvet Peppermint Crinkle Cookies are as pretty to look at as they are delicious to eat! This recipe has evolved over the years, and all that tweaking has resulted in a showstopper of a cookie!

CONTESTANT: BRETT YOUMANS

READING, PA

1 large egg

2 teaspoons espresso powder

1 teaspoon peppermint extract

½ cup + 2 tablespoons all-purpose flour

2 tablespoons unsweetened cocoa powder

1 teaspoon baking powder

1 teaspoon flaked sea salt

3½ tablespoons unsalted butter, room temperature

¾ cup light brown sugar

3½ ounces semisweet chocolate, melted

1½ tablespoons red food coloring

3½ ounces dark chocolate, roughly chopped

¼ cup granulated sugar

¼ cup confectioners' sugar

In a small bowl, whisk together the egg, espresso powder, and peppermint extract; set aside. In another small bowl, whisk together the flour, cocoa powder, baking powder, and salt; set aside.

Beat the butter and brown sugar with an electric mixer or stand mixer and beat until light and fluffy, about 3 minutes. Add the egg mixture and beat until well blended, about 2 minutes. Add the melted chocolate and food coloring and mix to combine. Gradually add the flour mixture and mix until combined and a smooth dough forms. Fold in the chopped chocolate. Cover with plastic wrap and refrigerate for 1 hour or until firm.

Heat the oven to 350°F. Line two large baking sheets with parchment paper or silicone baking mats.

Place the granulated and confectioners' sugars in separate shallow bowls. Portion the dough into tablespoon-size balls. First roll balls in the granulated sugar and then evenly coat in the confectioners' sugar. Place on prepared baking sheets, allowing room to spread. Bake 12–14 minutes, rotating the sheets halfway through, until the surface is cracked and the edges are set (cookies will appear underdone between the cracks). Let cool completely on baking sheets before serving.

TIRAMISU TRIPLE-CHOCOLATE
Sandwich Cookies

My family loves the traditional tiramisu dessert. This is what motivated me to create a special cookie with all the special ingredients of their favorite dessert. Because I use a lot of chocolate in my house, I knew that chocolate was going to be a major ingredient.

CONTESTANT: LINDA BONWILL
ENGLEWOOD, FL

Cookie Dough

- 2¼ cups all-purpose flour
- ½ cup cocoa powder
- ⅛ teaspoon salt
- 1½ cups granulated sugar
- 1 cup butter
- 1 large egg
- 1 teaspoon vanilla extract

Cream Filling

- 1½ cups confectioners' sugar
- ¼ cup strong brewed coffee
- 4 ounces mascarpone cheese, room temperature
- 2 tablespoons butter
- ½ teaspoon vanilla extract
- 12 ounces dark chocolate, melted, divided use

Make the cookie dough. Whisk together the flour, cocoa powder, and salt. In a separate bowl, with an electric mixer or stand mixer, blend the sugar and butter well. Add the egg and vanilla, and mix well.

Add the dry mixture to the wet mixture. Mix well to form dough. Divide the dough in half and wrap each half in plastic wrap. Refrigerate for 2 hours.

Preheat the oven to 350°F. Line baking sheets with parchment paper or silicone baking mats.

Roll out half of the dough to your preferred cookie thickness. Cut 2 inch circles and place on baking sheets. The circles may need to be chilled before handling. Re-chill the extra dough to roll and cut additional cookies. Repeat with the remaining dough. Bake cookies for 10 minutes. Cool completely before assembling.

Make the cream filling. Mix the confectioners' sugar, coffee, mascarpone, butter, vanilla, and 9 ounces of the melted chocolate.

Flip over half of the baked cookies. Add approximately ½ teaspoon of filling to the center of the flipped cookies and top with a plain cookie, pressing gently to create a sandwich. Make sure the two cookies are lined up evenly.

Drizzle the remaining 3 ounces of melted dark chocolate over tops of the assembled sandwich cookies.

DOUBLE-CHOCOLATE MINT TRUFFLE
Cookies

I've used this chocolate cookie dough base for many recipes over the course of many years. My six-year-old son absolutely loves the combination of peppermint and chocolate (he gets it from his mama), so I adapted the chocolate cookie dough base to include peppermint extract and added a chocolate mint truffle to the middle of each cookie. It's a little surprise when you bite into it! Thanks to the addition of cream cheese, the cookies are deliciously moist and fudgy, and the flavor is wonderful!

CONTESTANT: ERIN INDAHL-FINK
MANASSAS, VA

½ cup unsalted butter, room temperature

4 ounces cream cheese, room temperature

1¼ cups granulated sugar

1 egg

1 teaspoon peppermint extract

1½ cups all-purpose flour

½ cup cocoa powder

¾ teaspoon salt

¼ teaspoon baking powder

1 cup mini chocolate chips

18-24 mint truffle–filled chocolates

Preheat the oven to 350°F. Line baking sheets with parchment paper or silicone baking mats.

With an electric mixer or a stand mixer, cream together the butter and cream cheese. Add the sugar and cream together until fluffy. Add the egg and peppermint extract and mix until smooth and completely combined.

In a separate bowl, sift together the flour, cocoa powder, salt, and baking powder. Gradually add the dry ingredients to the wet ingredients, stopping to scrape down the sides of the bowl as needed. Pour the mini chips into a small bowl and unwrap the mint truffle chocolates.

Spoon out a teaspoon-size amount of dough and pat into a circle slightly larger than a quarter. Add a chocolate truffle to the center, and then add a tablespoon-size amount of dough on top of the truffle. Pat the dough together until the truffle is fully enclosed. The cookie will be about the size of a golf ball. Roll the cookie in the mini chips and place on the baking sheets. Repeat this process for the remaining dough.

Bake for 10–12 minutes. Let the cookies cool on the baking sheet for about 5 minutes before transferring to a wire rack.

Gluten-Free Snow-Capped
CHOCOLATE PEPPERMINT MACAROONS

My mother has a sweet tooth for coconut, my whole family loves chocolate, and peppermint patties top our list of favorite candies—this recipe was born out of love. Also, since life gets hectic with so much to do before the holidays, it's wonderful to have a simple-yet-delicious cookie recipe that can be made ahead and will keep fresh for up to 6 weeks if stored in an airtight container at room temperature. Since these cookies are gluten-free, I have finally created the perfect holiday cookie that all of my friends and loved ones can enjoy.

CONTESTANT: SARAH MEUSER
NEW MILFORD, CT

1   can (14 ounces) sweetened condensed milk

¼   cup unsweetened cocoa powder

¼   teaspoon pure peppermint extract

¼   teaspoon fine sea salt, divided use

14   ounces sweetened tender flake coconut

4   red-and-white-striped peppermint candies, chopped to a powder, divided use

Preheat the oven to 325°F. Line baking sheets with parchment paper or silicone baking mats.

In a large bowl, combine the sweetened condensed milk and cocoa powder and mix well with a spatula. Stir in the peppermint extract and ⅛ teaspoon of the sea salt. Add the coconut and mix well to combine.

For each cookie, fill 1.75 inch spring-loaded metal ice cream scoop with the mixture and drop onto prepared baking sheets, about 1 inch apart. Sprinkle the top with ⅛ teaspoon of the peppermint powder. Bake on the middle oven rack for 18–20 minutes or until the coconut begins to lightly brown.

In a small bowl, mix the remaining peppermint powder with the remaining ⅛ teaspoon sea salt and sprinkle over the tops of the warm cookies. Remove the cookies to wire racks. Cool completely before serving.

ULTIMATE CHOCOLATE CHIP
Cookies

I first made these cookies for my family to take with them to see a show in the park. I started with a basic chocolate chip cookie recipe and used better-quality chocolate and added in more flavors. I am a bit of a chocolate snob, so I use a combination of milk and dark chocolate bars instead of plain chocolate chips. I have always liked the combination of chocolate and orange, so I added orange extract. I included both walnuts and almonds because I could not decide which one to use. I added the coconut the second time I made these cookies to pair with the orange extract to give them a tropical feel.

CONTESTANT: JENNIFER ADAMS

PAMPA, TX

2¼ cups all-purpose flour
1 teaspoon baking soda
1 teaspoon salt
1 cup butter-flavored vegetable shortening
¾ cup granulated sugar
¾ cup packed brown sugar
1 teaspoon vanilla extract
1 teaspoon orange extract
2 large eggs
½ cup shredded coconut
½ cup chopped walnuts
½ cup chopped almonds
2.8 ounces milk chocolate, cut into small squares
2.8 ounces dark chocolate, cut into small squares

Preheat the oven to 350°F. Line baking sheets with parchment paper or silicone baking mats.

Combine the flour, baking soda, and salt in a bowl and set aside. Beat the shortening, sugars, vanilla, and orange extract with an electric mixer or stand mixer until creamy. Add the eggs, one at a time, beating well after each addition. Gradually beat in the flour mixture. Add the coconut, walnuts, and almonds and beat again.

Stir in the milk and dark chocolates with a spatula or wooden spoon. Scoop the cookies onto prepared baking sheets. Bake for 9–11 minutes or until golden brown.

CHOCOLATE MOCHA SALTED CARAMEL
Cookies

My husband is a big fan of the chocolate, coffee, and salted caramel combination, so I developed this cookie recipe with that in mind. I surprised him with these cookies on his birthday last year. He loved the flavor combination, and they were a big hit!

CONTESTANT: W. JIVRAJ
CENTREVILLE, PA

1 cup butter

⅔ cup cocoa powder

2 teaspoons instant coffee powder

2 eggs

2 cups granulated sugar

1 teaspoon vanilla extract

2 cups all-purpose flour

¾ teaspoon baking soda

½ teaspoon fleur de sel or sea salt + additional for sprinkling

1 tablespoon vanilla caramel coffee creamer powder

15 caramels, unwrapped and chopped

Preheat the oven to 350°F. Line a baking sheet with parchment paper or a silicone baking mat and set aside. In a small saucepan over medium heat, melt the butter. Add the cocoa powder and instant coffee powder. Whisk until smooth.

In a separate bowl, beat the eggs and sugar until pale and fluffy. Add the vanilla and mix well. Stir the butter mixture into the egg mixture. Whisk until well combined. Mix in the flour, baking soda, fleur de sel, and coffee creamer. Mix until just blended.

Drop rounded tablespoons of the cookie dough onto the baking sheet. Press 3–4 pieces of chopped caramels into each cookie and top with a sprinkle of fleur de sel. Bake for 10–11 minutes, and cool on a wire rack.

CHOCOLATE CHIP OATMEAL
Cookies

This recipe has been in our family for years. My grandmother would make these cookies for my mom, who would make them for us. It's a delicious, soft, and rich cookie.

CONTESTANT: VANESSA MATEO

MIAMI, FL

1 cup unsalted butter, softened

1 cup granulated sugar

1 cup light brown sugar

2 large eggs

1 teaspoon vanilla extract

2 cups all-purpose flour

1 teaspoon baking powder

1 teaspoon baking soda

½ teaspoon salt

2 cups old-fashioned rolled oats

4 ounces milk chocolate, chopped using a food processor

6 ounces milk chocolate chips

6 ounces semisweet chocolate chips

Preheat the oven to 350°F. Line a baking sheet with parchment paper or a silicone baking mat.

With an electric mixer or stand mixer fitted with a whisk attachment, cream the butter and sugars together. Add the eggs, one at a time, mixing well after each addition. Add the vanilla.

In a separate bowl, combine the flour, baking powder, baking soda, and salt. Add the dry ingredients to the butter mixture and stir to combine. Add the rolled oats and chopped chocolate. Mix well. Fold in the chocolate chips by hand.

Scoop 1–1½ inch round balls and place them on the baking sheet, about 1 inch apart. Bake for 10–12 minutes until the bottoms of the cookies brown.

INDEX